Church and State in Your Community

CHRISTIAN PERSPECTIVES
ON SOCIAL PROBLEMS

Gayraud S. Wilmore, *General Editor*

Church and State in Your Community

by

ELWYN A. SMITH

Philadelphia

THE WESTMINSTER PRESS

LIBRARY OF CONGRESS CATALOG CARD No. 63–7263

PRINTED IN THE UNITED STATES OF AMERICA

Contents

Contents

Foreword

THIS BOOK IS ONE OF SEVERAL TO APPEAR DURING THE next few years in a series entitled Christian Perspectives on Social Problems. This is an attempt to meet a challenge from an exceedingly robust minority of laymen for brief, readable analyses of cultural problems from a theological perspective. It is intended to help them *think theologically* about some of the exasperatingly difficult problems of society, both the issues which relate to life in America and those which link this nation to the destiny of the world.

Recent researches on family life have found laymen obsessed with "loving, happy relations" in the family, with child-rearing and personal problems of status and adjustment, but with little comprehension of how private troubles bisect public issues. This curious fascination with selfhood to the neglect of neighborhood is not, however, a universal malaise of Protestantism. A minority, perhaps, but a minority that refuses to be lightly regarded by ecclesiastical officialdom, is demanding to know the meaning of events of our day for the Christian faith and to demonstrate the critical and renewing power of faith in secular society.

It is to these doughty men and women that the several volumes of the Christian Perspectives on Social Problems series are directed, and it is hoped that they will not only make for an unsettling reading experience but will provide stimulating material for small-group study and discussion. To that end, questions for discussion are appended to each of the books as starters for fruitful controversy.

The relation of the church to the civil order has been debated by theologians since the fourth century A.D., but Americans are experiencing a new awareness of its importance. This is partly due, undoubtedly, to increased interest in the nature of the church; particularly in the relation of sacred institutions to secular institutions, the church life of Sunday to the rest of the week that is so dominated by the power of the modern state.

But American concern about church-state relations has also been due to more partisan and practical interests. For example, recent attempts to exploit the advantage in international politics of alignment with the Vatican, increased ecclesiastical power in public affairs, and proposals for governmental aid to parochial schools. Protestant laymen have reacted negatively and noisily to all three issues.

Professor Smith, of the Pittsburgh Theological Seminary, offers here a positive approach to some of the practical problems arising across the nation in communities seeking clarity in this perplexing and complex area of church-state relations. His own answers are tentative, exploratory, and controversial and, as such, calculated to provoke study and discussion in the churches.

The author is chairman of the Special Committee of the 174th General Assembly of The United Presbyterian Church in the U.S.A. whose report on church-state relations was received for study with great interest and promises to be the focus of extended debate in that denomination and in American Protestantism generally.

GAYRAUD S. WILMORE

Pittsburgh, Pennsylvania

Chapter I

The Ordeal of Hightown, U.S.A.

THE PURPOSE OF THIS BOOK IS TO CLARIFY THE precise bearing of the general problem of church-state relations on the actual situations that occur in American communities. While discussion of constitutional and religious issues cannot be omitted, this book starts where discussion of church and state almost always starts—in a community actually trying to make a decision. The community we have chosen was trying to decide on the place of Christmas observances in its public-school system. We have called it Hightown, U.S.A. Except for names, the report is wholly factual and is based on a careful on-the-spot investigation.

Behind the bitterness that divided the citizens of Hightown in the Christmas season of 1960 lay fundamental questions that few of them could answer clearly. What does the American principle of separation of church and state imply? How should it affect Hightown's long-established community traditions? What is "religious" and what is not? Most observers of Hightown agree that the lack of public understanding of basic questions contributed materially to the confusion that prevented both the town's leaders and its citizens from reaching a decision without destructive conflict.

American churches are touched by civil authority in a

variety of ways. Church property is tax-exempt; church colleges are eligible for Government loans for buildings; ministers serving as chaplains in the Armed Forces are paid by the Government; church-related hospitals and welfare agencies receive support from tax funds under specific contract arrangements. In these matters, church and state are not so much separated as harmonized in well-defined ways.

On the other hand, no church may be established by law; Government may not interfere in the religious life of any citizen; church-related primary and secondary schools may not receive public aid; religious indoctrination may not take place in public schools; weekday religious education may not be conducted on public-school premises or during normal school hours. Here a "wall of separation" has been built. Why at these points and not others?

The base line from which Americans work in determining the relation of church and state was drawn by the authors of the First Amendment to the national Constitution. "Congress shall make no law respecting an establishment of religion, or prohibiting the free exercise thereof." Furthermore, freedom of speech, press, and assembly were guaranteed. All of these are important aspects of religious freedom, since church and individuals speak, write, and educate the young in group assemblies. The Constitution, therefore, clearly protects religious liberty. Does it also call for general separation of church and state?

Another problem: "religious liberty" is guaranteed by the First Amendment, but what about "moral liberty"? Religion and morals travel together in American history, but the line between them is sometimes difficult to draw. For example, the Mormons, in an earlier generation, held that polygamy was a matter of religion and demanded the protection of the First Amendment for its practice. Nevertheless, polygamy was forbidden by the Supreme Court as outside the bounds of the nation's conception of morality. Pacifism is also a moral position, yet the Supreme Court agrees that it is closely enough allied with religion to furnish conscientious objectors with immunity from arrest *provided* their reasons are religious. In the current American view, in short, some pacifism is religious and therefore protected while the rest is not. Can so tenuous a line really be drawn?

It is obvious to students of church-state relations in America that separation cannot mean the same thing for all the manifold questions that arise as churches and religious opinions enter into relation with government. It is also obvious that the principle of separation of church and state is an essential guarantee of religious liberty in America and cannot be abandoned, for all its ambiguities, without a fundamental change in the public tradition. The problem is to understand what the separation of church and state actually means in precise relationship to laws, customs, and traditions that prevail in the cities and towns of the United States.

It Happened in Hightown

Here is the story of how one American community stumbled unwittingly into a public schism that profoundly shocked every person in it and left gnawing fear that it could happen again.

Early in 1960, a full nine months before the outbreak of the controversy, a group of Hightown citizens gathered to discuss the place of religion in their public schools. Most of these persons were non-Protestant and all of them doubted that the prominence of Christmas observances in the schools could be defended either on educational or Constitutional grounds. Several were parents of children who had been embarrassed by the Christmas programming. One Jewish child, for example, had been asked to take part in a Nativity play; teachers occasionally asked that children who had attended Sunday school should stand. The Christmas pageantry seemed to this group to have a decidedly Protestant character and even to border on worship. Art projects depended heavily on New Testament themes; Christian prayer was being offered in the classroom, and sometimes children were asked to kneel.

At first these citizens had no specific course of action in mind. They did not object to the singing of Christmas carols, which they regarded as traditional rather than specifically religious. Furthermore, they had no desire to secularize the school system by forcing Hightown into a rigid application of church-state separation. They were Quakers, Unitarians, and Jews, and they wanted their children relieved of embarrassment and their schools to leave religious teaching to the churches.

The group decided to try to modify public-school practices by speaking privately with members of the school board. It was charged during the peaceless Christmas season of 1960 that these discussions represented secret and improper intervention in established public custom.

For some time the administrators of Hightown's public school had been uneasy about the amounts of time devoted to preparing Christmas programs. Neither the members of the school board nor the school administrators had any personal quarrel with the customs of the schools, but they recognized that the protest of the non-Protestant parents was justified on both educational and Constitutional grounds. In several meetings with principals in the late summer and fall of 1960, therefore, the superintendent of schools urged that religious observances in the schools be tactfully de-emphasized.

Custom could not be so easily changed. As December approached the usual extensive Christmas preparations got under way. On December 3 the superintendent repeated his counsel to the principals. Why this should have produced an emotional explosion remains a mystery to many residents of Hightown to this day. But an explosion there was.

The match was struck by a handful of principals and teachers; the first flash occurred in a single school. The principal involved reacted angrily to the remarks of the superintendent and instructed his teachers to remove Christmas posters and decorations immediately. On the evening of December 3 several hundred children arrived at home with their Christmas drawings in their hands, tearful and confused. The parents' reaction was instantaneous. "What in the name of common sense is going on here?" "Who is responsible for this?" "Is the school board against Christmas?"

Another community might not have taken fire. Why did the question of religious observances in public schools ignite Hightown?

The reaction against the Hightown school board was not the handiwork of any organized extremist group in the city. Such a group soon took form, but the reaction was itself spontaneous. Those who know the history of Hightown remember that in the 1930's the Ku-Klux Klan had marked out Roman Catholics, Jews, and Negroes as a threat. In the 1950's a series of trials and appeals had given wide publicity to a band of Communists accused of conspiring to overthrow the Government. A handful of people in Hightown, generally regarded as fanatical, had maintained a steady drumbeat of criticism of the Federal Government. The argument that Communism is winning everywhere in the world and threatening American public life through subversion had been persistently presented in Hightown through private mailings by disturbed citizens. The editorial policy of the newspaper was consistently moderate, however, and its news coverage notably fair. Hightown had a small group devoted to the exposure of Communism but no local chapter of the John Birch Society, although its publications were persistently quoted.

What might have been no more than a public question calling for an explanation by the school board became a state of hysteria. Who had subverted the school board? The most alarmed were the first to write letters to the newspaper. There was virtually no support for the school board.

At first, the school board believed that full explanation would satisfy the parents of Hightown, but a public meeting called on December 12 failed dismally. A last-minute effort to marshal Protestant sentiment behind the school board decision backfired when the clergyman appointed to read a Council of Churches statement of support launched into a strong attack on the document. The chairman of the school board was unable to control the meeting. The most extreme charges of Communism, atheism, subversion, and hatred of Christianity were aired, and at certain moments the twelve hundred people present verged on violence. By midnight the fair field of this community had been sown with a hateful seed that was flourishing a year later.

Both the advocates of a cutback of Christmas observances in the schools and the opponents of change had prepared for the public meeting of December 12. The clergyman who attacked the school board had gathered his supporters at his church beforehand and in concert they moved into the front rows as the meeting began. Less formally and, as it turned out, less effectively, the advocates of more separation of religion from public education planned their own role. Representatives of the staunchly anti-Communist American Civil Liberties Union appeared in Hightown, leading a few to declare excitedly that organized pro-Communist forces had invaded from the big city.

The gross intemperance of the public meeting created a reaction favorable to the school board. Some church people began to feel that the case for Christianity was in poor hands. One woman published a letter stating that the Christ she knew would have been humiliated by the conduct of his Christians that night. She dissociated herself from the "Christian Americans" and apologized to the non-Christian community for her personal failure to understand that their liberties were not being sufficiently respected in the schools. The local paper at first had severely criticized the school board for poorly interpreting its ruling to the public; it now voiced confidence in the members of the school board, praised its previous accomplishments, and urged that the town promptly take the road to reconciliation.

By December 12 five Hightown men had obtained an injunction forbidding the school board to carry out its directive to de-emphasize religion in the schools. Upon protest of the school board, the injunction was dismissed. Shortly after, the same five plaintiffs sued the school board for infringement of the right of their children to free exercise of their religion in the public schools. Amid dire warnings by the plaintiffs, this suit was later dropped.

The viewpoints of these plaintiffs differed widely. One professed no religious commitment of any kind; two were church members, only one of these active in church affairs. The common ground among them was fear of the destruction of an American tradition. Several had been persistent critics of the United Nations, the National Council of the Churches of Christ in the United States of America, the State Department, and both major political parties. Their uneasiness was shared by a substantial minority of the Protestant clergymen of Hightown.

An election of school board members was due in March, 1961, and the Christian Americans formed a committee to oppose the reelection of the candidates who had participated in the school board decision to cut back religious observances. Mailings, paid advertising, and radio spots argued that these candidates "hated Christianity." But Hightown had been profoundly shocked by the bitterness of their Christmastide, 1960, and the attack failed.

During January, 1961, a group of particularly well-educated citizens of Hightown—clergymen, journalists, professors, scientists—formed a Committee of Inquiry to frame a basis for settlement. This committee was the only body that undertook specific study of church-state separation. In February, the school board appointed a committee of its own to recommend terms of reconciliation. This body heard spokesmen for all viewpoints. The careful work of the Committee of Inquiry made a sound contribution to the document issued by the board's own committee of reconciliation in July, 1961.

Private agitation continued while the school board was seeking a policy of pacification. Mimeographed literature and anonymous threats by telephone kept Hightown on edge. Nevertheless, in the school board election in March the public decisively defeated all candidates for the school board supported by critics of the decision to de-emphasize religious observances.

Finally, in September, 1961, the newly elected school board announced its policy. While it gave no cause to fear that an irreligious spirit had seized the schools, it maintained the ground taken earlier by the board. A cultural and educational approach to religion in the schools was approved and the Christian heritage acknowledged as part of the national tradition, but religious indoctrination was forbidden. Seasonal programming was permitted provided it was nonsectarian and educationally valuable. Singing of carols was approved; student freedom to refuse to participate in seasonal programs was affirmed; and voluntary prayer by students in extracurricular activity was allowed.

What Kind of Town?

What was settled in Hightown, U.S.A.? Did the price in friction purchase some understanding of basic issues? The specific dispute of December, 1960, over religious observances in the schools was successfully compromised. At Christmas, 1961, the editor of the town paper received no letters protesting the settlement. Weary of its strife, Hightown refused further debate. It is a chastened community. It has fewer illusions about itself.

Does Hightown understand why it fell into division?

Certainly its people know that Hightown is not what they thought it was. Until the Second World War, this quiet community was preponderantly Protestant and largely free of the anxieties that afflict Americans experiencing social change. Hightown knows now that it must come to terms with newcomers who are not willing to accept the majority mood of the years before 1945. Hightown had always had a few Jews, Roman Catholics, and Negroes. Motivated by deeply emotional fear of anti-Semitism, older Jewish residents opposed the efforts of the newcomers in early 1960 to alter school customs. While the newer Jewish community is far from orthodox in faith, it desires to identify itself as Jewish. Hightown discovered its Jews in a new way. One result, as predicted by the older Jews, was an unmistakable rise of anti-Semitism.

The Roman Catholic community stood aloof from the debate. Although there are parochial schools in Hightown, substantial numbers of Roman Catholics attend public schools. Individual Roman Catholic laymen participated in the reconciling efforts, but the priests made no public statements. The Roman Catholic community did not ask for a change and, in contrast with the new Jewish residents, tacitly refused to identify itself as a subcommunity.

Between 1945 and 1960, in short, Hightown had

ceased to be a homogeneous "Protestant" community and followed the well-marked path toward religious pluralism. More than before, although still not in proportion to the national distribution, the pattern of the nation has come to Hightown: several religions and cultures seeking ways to live at peace with one another. From one point of view, the dispute over religious observances in the public school was Hightown's first faltering step in the direction of diversified urban culture. If some of the residents of Hightown have not yet learned how to live with their new neighbors, they know that they must. Some still feel that this new America is not really American at all. But most know that cultural pluralism is American in its own way and that Hightown must achieve a more realistic self-understanding.

Chapter II

Hightown's View of Church and State

DOES HIGHTOWN UNDERSTAND THE GENERAL PROBLEM of how to relate religion to civil authority any better than before?

The majority probably understands church-state relations no better. The committee appointed by the school board found it necessary to refute at length the widespread feeling that the majority is entitled to what it wants, regardless of minority protest. Only a few particularly well-informed citizens understand that pluralism, separation of church and state, a secular public order, and the defense of the rights of minorities compose an American pattern. Very few of its citizens see Hightown's troubles as a clash between two equally American traditions: the rural Western tradition of the homogeneous Protestant community versus the new urban tradition of many peoples adjusting their differences.

No actual dispute concerning church and state includes all its numerous applications, yet disputes on all sorts of church-state issues demand the successful application of a lesson that Americans have learned from their own history: the separation of church and state is this nation's best guarantee of religious liberty, civil justice, and the vigor of the churches.

Many church-state problems are national rather than

local. They concern Federal legislation (for example, loans to church-related colleges) or policy in Federally administered agencies (for example, maintenance of chaplains in the Armed Forces). Other church-state problems, however, appear in local communities and most of them cannot be settled anywhere else except by appeal to courts. Among these are public-school policy; zoning appeals by churches; liquor control laws; the use of parks, courthouse lawns, and other public properties for religious displays; the evaluation of the fitness of candidates for local offices on the basis of religious affiliation; the dispensing of birth control information in municipal or county hospitals and clinics; Sunday closing laws; state laws governing marriage, divorce, and adoption; and exemption of church properties from real estate taxes. Disputes highly dangerous to the integrity of any community can break out around any of these questions. All of them demand some grasp of the meaning of the separation of church and state and the way it can solve rather than magnify problems.

Although one or two of its citizens argued that the city park should not display the Christian cross at the Easter season, Hightown encountered the church-state problem in the familiar costume of the public-school question. Yet the issue of church-state relations wears the garb of all the above-listed questions. If Hightown had been forced to probe any one of them earlier, it might have found its public-school dispute less destructive. If Hightown can now understand the general issue at the heart of its most troubled Christmas season, it will be better prepared for any other disagreement involving church and state, in whatever guise it appears.

What Is Meant by "Church"?

It is rather difficult to separate church and state until we know what the two words mean. Theologians differ on the meaning of the word "church," but in American public usage it means all churches, denominations, sects, cults, or other societies, Christian or not, that profess religious purposes. In constitutional debate, "church" is a collective term for any organized expression of religion or all of them taken together. Just how general the word "church" can get can be seen in the fact that no actual church organization was in the least implicated in the religious observances in the schools. The churches had not urged them; the people expected them. When ministers participated they did so by invitation and without compensation. Organized churches had virtually nothing to do with religion in the town's schools—yet it was a church-state debate just the same! In American usage, "church" includes "sectarian religious practices."

Once the battle was joined, however, the organized churches spoke up. In reality, it is always some particular body or group of bodies that speaks for the church. In Hightown this was complicated. The local Council of Churches wrote a statement, but not all the congregations in Hightown are members of that Council and not all the clergymen in the Council agreed with the statement. A group of ministers publicized their opposition to the Council's deliverance and worked in general harmony with the supporters of Christian Americanism, many of whom were not churchmen at all.

Furthermore, individual congregations stated their own views. The elders of the First Presbyterian Church, for example, adopted this minute: "We affirm our belief in the Constitutional provision for the separation of church and state. We oppose any teaching of 'sectarian' religious doctrine within the public-school system. However, we affirm that religion as identified with ethical and moral development and as implicit within the teaching of art, drama, history, music, etc., can and must be taught by the public-school system in the communication of our national heritage."

Over their own names and speaking only for themselves, two Hightown ministers published thoughtful letters warning against the entanglement of the Christian faith with Americanism.

So it will always be, especially among Protestants who so highly value their liberty to differ with one another and with everyone else. Had the leaders of the Hightown Council of Churches been able to persuade both its members and all religious bodies outside its membership to join in a single statement, Hightown might have heard a less uncertain sound issuing from the church. Even if they had agreed, however, the churches of Hightown could have spoken only for themselves; there would remain the whole body of Christians elsewhere in the world for whom they could have spoken only indirectly at best.

While Christians may view the church as one, the cold fact is that it does not actually exist as one but as many. Under these conditions, Americans may be excused when they wonder about the divisions in the church. They still find it confusing to have to ask what all the churches, denominations, sects, cults, and other religious associations think.

How About the State?

As far as Hightown was concerned, the "state" was its school board. Obviously, the state is much more than a school board—a considerable number of young Americans meet it as a draft board! But in the Hightown dispute the school board was the body invested by law with the right to organize, finance, and administer a public-school system. In another kind of church-state problem—a disagreement, let us say, over dissemination of birth control information in a county hospital—the voice of the state would be heard from a hospital administrator.

"State" often means simply "government" in one form or another. "Civil authority" is a better word because it distinguishes authority based on laws enacted by the whole public from authority based on the agreement of members of a private organization such as the Elks Club, a business corporation, or a church. These may run their own affairs but no one else's.

When Americans use the word "state," therefore, they do not mean that the whole reality of American society, its private organizations and public ideals, is expressed primarily by means of government. In Germany in the last century there grew up the philosophy of "statism": that the German state was the supreme expression of the whole of German life and thought. This is not the American view. The government is only one means by which Americans accomplish their purposes; power is deliberately divided between government and other sources of influence, such as the press, churches, schools, and an immense variety of groups. While the commonweal is the sphere within which law operates, in liberal democracy large areas of the common welfare are only slightly touched by law.

CHURCH-STATE RELATIONS

Church-state relations in their entirety involve the relating of all religions and religious bodies to all the varied forms in which civil authority exists in America. As a practical matter, it is simpler than that. Church-state relations in Hightown in December, 1960, meant only how much and what kind of Christmas programming should be permitted in its public school. The decision of the school board was specific: some but not too much, and whatever there was must be nonsectarian—that is, not offensive to non-Christians.

We know about religion in Hightown's public schools, but what about the separation of church and state in Hightown? If the question is asked in general, Hightown gave no answer. The city was not engaged in a study program; it was seeking the way out of a bitter quarrel. But certain views of church-state relations are implicit in the decision made by the Hightown school board.

First, Hightown apparently believes that it is possible to distinguish between a public Christmas that belongs to everybody and a Christian Christmas that belongs only to Christian believers. One of the 1960 Christmas pageants in the Hightown schools had lines in it that taught the deity of Christ—or so it seemed to those who questioned it. They felt that such a program belongs only to the Christian churches. However, the Wise Men, the Bethlehem scene, and even the carols—not to speak of jingle bells and fir trees—in Hightown's opinion make up a kind of American traditional Christmas to which non-Christians there do not strongly object. So Christmas, 1961, in Hightown had carols and crèches, but its Nativity plays did not call Jesus the Son of God or Mary the mother of God. All specifically doctrinal (i.e., sectarian) suggestions were combed out.

Whom does this solution really suit?

Although no protest was raised in 1961 by Jewish, Unitarian, and other non-Christian groups in Hightown, some continue to question the propriety of a manger scene in public schools. From another angle, thoughtful churchmen are asking themselves whether a celebration of Christmas from which all reference to the divine character of Jesus has been expunged can serve any useful purpose from the Christian point of view. The only people pleased by Hightown's all-American Christmas are those who think very indefinitely about Christianity or who do not care about religion at all, but who regard traditional Christmas celebrations in public schools as an important way to make the children really American.

A further implication may be seen. The Hightown decision seems to suggest that while Christianity may belong first of all to those who believe it religiously, it is also the common property of all who adhere to it culturally. There are, in short, two Christianities just as there are two Christmases. Nonsectarian Christianity is legitimate within publicly supported institutions; religious Christianity is legitimate only in churches and homes.

Few will deny that Christianity in its many forms is an important thread in American history. Even the little spooks of Halloween got their start in a Christian tradition! Thanksgiving was first celebrated by men and women who prayed to a Christ whom they believed divine, and Easter makes little sense as a resurrection event apart from Christian belief in the divine nature of the One who rose from death. Yet all these are also a part of the American heritage, even though many modern Americans do not pray and believe as their forebears did. On that ground, the Hightown school board agreed that the religious festivals should be explained in the public schools.

"Explained" was their word. Sharp questions from teenagers, it is true, can carry a teacher from history into theology in a jiffy. Still, the distinction between explaining religious beliefs and advocating them can be made. It certainly makes better sense to distinguish between explaining and advocating religious positions than to drain the blood out of religion in order to make it universally acceptable. But if religious commitment is deep and widespread in a community, another solution may be needed. The religiously committed do not want the doctrines they live by simply explained. They want them advocated by people who believe them.

As matters stand, separation of church and state in Hightown boils down to a separation of religion into two kinds: nonsectarian public religion and religious religion. Only a handful of Protestants are worried lest the impression be left with Hightown's children that Christianity is something merely nominal.

THE COMMUNITY TRADITION

Every community has to decide for itself how to bring the principle of separation of church and state into working harmony with its established traditions. In Hightown, those traditions were Protestant-American. For that reason, when the contest was joined, the Protestant-American tradition in the town asserted itself very strongly.

Hightown continues to believe that the state as well as the church possesses a generally Protestant character. The steps of separation undertaken in the Hightown schools did not eliminate Protestant religion altogether from the civil sphere; the public schools were not radically secularized. Had that happened, all mention of religion would have been excluded, perhaps at the expense of education itself. Other communities have moved much farther toward complete secularization by forbidding religious observances altogether and putting instruction in religion off the campus. In Hightown, "state" clearly includes some religion.

It might be argued that the survival of religion of a sort in the Hightown schools means that the school board did not really separate church and state at all. But the fact remains that a change was made; and the change did take place in schools financed and administered by civil authority. Whatever Hightown schools are, therefore, represents a part of Hightown's idea of the state.

The Hightown view of the state implicitly affirms that religion is inherent in the state; that private convictions cannot be wholly separated from the public stance; and that so long as religious organizations are not involved in any specific linkage with the state no breach of the separation principle is entailed in the presence of religion (as Hightown defines it) in public education.

Chapter III

The Nation's View of Church and State

THE JUSTICES OF THE SUPREME COURT OF THE UNITED States do their thinking about church and state from the same standpoint as the Hightown school board: they start with a specific problem, try to align it with the Constitution of the United States, and come up with a decision suitably seasoned with realism.

While the Supreme Court has not expounded any general theory of church-state relations, the justices have reasoned very seriously on a number of legal appeals that involve problems of church and state. More than the Hightown school board or, for that matter, any local civil authority, they try to be consistent on basic issues. They do not always succeed; justices come and go and the Court sees church-state relations differently from time to time. Nevertheless, the Supreme Court has created a body of opinion that guides the whole nation.

The Court's thinking on church and state may be divided into reasonably strong separationism and what may be called, in a phrase of Justice William O. Douglas, "common sense" separation. All justices at all times have accepted the separation of church from state, but they have differed on what it should mean in specific cases.

21

STRONG SEPARATIONISM

Roger Williams, the refugee from the Massachusetts Bay Colony, was the first to speak of a "wall of separation" and his phrase was used by Thomas Jefferson. While President, Jefferson wrote to a group of Connecticut Baptists: "Believing with you that religion is a matter which lies solely between man and his God, that he owes account to none other for his faith or his worship, that the legislative powers of government reach actions only and not opinions, I contemplate with sovereign reverence that act of the whole American people which declared that their legislature should 'Make no law respecting an establishment of religion, or prohibiting the free exercise thereof,' thus building a wall of separation between church and state."

Jefferson wanted the wall high and solid. He had been through a struggle before the Revolution to prevent the Virginia government from levying taxes to support clergymen. Baptists and Presbyterians, who disliked the established English Church in Virginia, supported him. Jefferson even refused to proclaim a national day of prayer, so scrupulous was he to avoid all interference in the rituals of religion and the sphere of the church.

In our time, the Supreme Court has four times spelled out the following definition of the wall of separation. "The establishment of religion clause of the First Amendment means at least this: neither a state nor the Federal Government can set up a church. Neither can pass laws which aid one religion, aid all religions, or prefer one religion over another. Neither can force nor influence a person to go to or to remain away from church against his will or force him to profess a belief or disbelief of any religion. No person can be punished for entertaining or professing religious beliefs or disbeliefs, for church attendance or nonattendance. No tax in any amount, large or small, can be levied to support any religious activities or institutions, whatever they may be called, or whatever form they may adopt to teach or practice religion. Neither a state nor the Federal Government can, openly or secretly, participate in the affairs of any religious organizations or groups and vice versa. In the words of Jefferson, the clause against establishment of religion by law was intended to erect 'a wall of separation between church and state.' "

On the other side of the fence—the question is how *strict* separation should be—stand opinions such as those of Justices Douglas and Jackson. "There cannot be the slightest doubt that the First Amendment reflects the philosophy that church and state should be separated," wrote Justice Douglas in 1951. "And so far as interference with the 'free exercise' of religion and 'establishment' of religion are concerned, the separation must be complete and unequivocal. . . . The First Amendment, however, does not say that in every and all respects there shall be separation of church and state. Rather it studiously defines the manner . . . in which there shall be no concert or union or dependency one on the other. That is the common sense of the matter. Otherwise the state and religion would be aliens to each other—hostile, suspicious, and even unfriendly. Churches could not be required to pay even property taxes. Municipalities would not be permitted to render police or fire protection to religious groups. Policemen who helped parishioners into their places of worship would violate the Constitution. Prayers in our legislative halls; the appeals to the Almighty in the messages of the Chief Executive; the proclamation making Thanksgiving a holiday; 'so help me God' in our courtroom oaths—these and all other references to the Almighty that run through our laws, our public rituals, our ceremonies would be flouting the First Amendment. A fastidious atheist or agnostic could even object to the supplication

21360

with which the Court opens each session: 'God save the United States and this Honorable Court.' " Justice Douglas protests against the conversion of the political principle of the separation of church and state into the assertion that religion is—or must be made—wholly distinct from public life.

There is a very important difference between these two which is sometimes obscured. "Separation means separation," wrote Justice Frankfurter in 1948, "not something less. Jefferson's metaphor . . . speaks of a 'wall of separation,' not a fine line easily overstepped. . . . 'The great American principle of eternal separation'—Elihu Root's phrase bears repetition—is one of the vital reliances of our Constitutional system for securing unities among our people stronger than our diversities. It is the Court's duty to enforce this principle in its full integrity. We renew our conviction that 'we have staked the very existence of our country on the faith that complete separation between the state and religion is best for the state and best for religion.' If nowhere else, in the relation between church and state, 'good fences make good neighbors.' " (Joseph Tussman, *The Supreme Court on Church and State*. Oxford University Press, 1962.)

Justice Frankfurter's insistence that civil power should never become entangled with the policies or politics of religious groups does not mean that religious groups may not try to win others to their own views; it does mean that they may not use civil power in order to accomplish it. Voluntary groups in the United States, religious or not, may argue and persuade all they wish. But no religious group can enact law or use other political means to deprive citizens outside their fellowship of their freedom to think, worship, and act as they please within the bounds of laws applicable to all persons.

The distinction between "religion" and "church" is a matter of some moment in determining what is meant by separation of church and state. If the word "religion" be taken to mean not organized religious groups or religious manifestations—its common meaning—but religious conviction itself, to demand 'complete separation between the state and religion' is to say that the President of the United States, its legislators, administrators, judges, and other public servants cannot adhere to any religion at all —or if they do, that they must make a separation within their own minds between their religious faith and their way of thinking and performing their public responsibilities. This is an impossible demand. Few men know themselves well enough to sort their ideas into pigeonholes labeled "religious" and "nonreligious."

To demand that religion (rather than "church") be separated from the state is really to say that religion is a private matter which can have no proper bearing on social and political affairs. It is to say that there exists a non-religious social and political philosophy adequate to the situation of the American people. A substantial number of intelligent Americans believe both of these propositions. But a large number of equally responsible Americans who ardently support separation of church and state utterly disagree with them.

COMMON SENSE SEPARATION

As questionable as the underlying assumptions of strong separationism may be, the dictum of Justice Douglas that "we are a religious people" also has its problems. If we are a religious people, what religion? President Eisenhower gave a completely candid answer to that question: "Our government makes no sense unless it is founded in a deeply felt religious faith—and I don't care what it is." (Quoted from Will Herberg's *Protestant, Catholic, Jew,* p. 97. Doubleday & Co., Inc., 1955.) His advice has been scorned by some because it leaves so many questions unanswered; but in actuality, Mr. Eisenhower was close to describing the way things stand in America today. His remark was not much different from the statement of Justice Douglas, who is widely praised by many who find Mr. Eisenhower too ingenuous.

There may be a few who would like to fix a particular religion or church on America. This charge is often made against the Roman Catholic Church. Spain or Paraguay, two thoroughly clericalized societies, are cited as embodying the ideal Roman Catholic political order. A few Roman Catholics who are wholly out of touch with American history may cherish such hopes, but there are influential Roman Catholic theorists like Father John Courtney Murray, S.J., who would consider such a turn of affairs in America a disaster for the Roman Catholic Church.

A more substantial question raised by the axiom that "we are a religious people" was the one debated in Hightown. No one there wanted to destroy religion, in or out of public education; but some did feel it necessary to remove the sectarian element from the schools. Is the distinction between religion and sectarianism useful? For public purposes, Hightown defined religion as the moral teaching accepted by the majority of the townsmen. Religious religion, as we have called it, was eliminated from the schools. This adds up to the equation: sectarianism is religious religion.

The alternative to sectarianism is all American religion. What is that?

Just this—we are "one nation, under God, . . . with liberty and justice for all." A nation like ours, this public religion suggests, is the work not of man but of God. God is the Guarantor of American liberties. In Hightown, the traditional observance of Christmas in the public schools all of a sudden became a symbol of the "nation under God." Those who wanted sectarian practices removed from the schools found themselves confronted by the charge that it was not sectarianism they were opposing but America's national foundations.

The misunderstanding contained in this feeling was too deeply buried in the consciousness of the partisans to Hightown's quarrel to be clarified quickly. What one called a sectarian doctrine another called fundamental religiousness. In a sense, Justice Frankfurter's preoccupation with the need for separation was pitted against Justice Douglas' observation that Americans are a religious people.

NONRELIGIOUS AND RELIGIOUS APPROACHES TO SEPARATION

Not only among Supreme Court justices but among other Americans as well, there are two distinct ways of thinking about separation of church and state. We will call them the "nonreligious line" and the "religious line" of thought.

The nonreligious line is willing to disbar religion from any role in the making of law or administrative decisions, even in the form of the personal moral convictions of legislators and executives. This is not a new viewpoint. In the time of the French religious wars, (1562–1598) no adjustment between the Roman Catholics and Huguenots seemed possible, and one group of French political philosophers concluded that government should be conducted wholly on principles of expediency. They were called "politiques": policy men.

Some American policy men, like the French, are not personally without religious faith, but they all believe that politics is a science with its own rules. A public executive who follows them can maintain civil tranquillity and public safety, the goals of politics.

Along the nonreligious line of thought, separation of church and state means that a public figure ought to introduce into his thought and argument only considerations that are politically useful. If a Roman Catholic politique were President, for example, the non-Catholic public could be assured that his personal religious and moral conviction would never affect the decisions of his office—only his knowledge of the rules of politics. If public administration could be reduced to an objective science—and if Americans could be convinced that other things believed by their governors were *really* being excluded from politics —a country inhabited by people of many faiths need never fall into disputes over religion in public affairs. There would be no religion into public affairs.

How about the religious interpretation of separation of church and state?

In the first place, it is realistic. Pseudoreligion and national patriotic mythology are not all there is of religion in this country. Discount, as we may wish, the seriousness of many millions of religiously affiliated Americans, there is still a vast number who are completely in earnest about religion, not all of them church members and some of them occupying positions of great public importance. Justice Douglas' generalization, difficulties of definition notwithstanding, contains truth. The nonreligious view of church-state separation is not likely soon to become the people's view. It is noteworthy that politiques who run for public office in America generally conceal their secularism under a convenient church affiliation.

The religious line of thinking on church-state separation believes that it is impossible and undesirable for a religiously committed man to keep his religion for Sundays. The more highly developed his religion, the more it will pervade his entire thought and life. Here the impact of a candidate's religion on his public office will be felt. Does his religiousness bind him to jail everyone who disagrees with him? Then his religion makes him unfit for public office. Does his religion forbid him to wage war in defense of the nation? Then he cannot be Commander

in Chief of the Army, Navy, and Air Force. Does his
religious commitment mean that he believes God expects
him to give himself completely to his job? Nations are led
through suffering to triumph by such men. Does his religious commitment bind his conscience to defend the freedom of all citizens to make up their minds about religious
faith without intervention by civil authority? This kind of
religion may be more effective in making him a good President than his solemn oath to uphold the Constitution.

While personally religious men may make very strong
public executives, we can see a very weak side in the
religious interpretation of church-state relations. When
religion slips over to the side of the state and becomes a
general public possession, a kind of national myth, it is
falsified. Such religion, in short, loses its center, the religious relationship of men and societies to God. At its
worst, watered-down public religion has produced some of
the rankest weeds of our national experience: the American Protectionist Association, the Ku-Klux Klan, the Christian Anti-Communist Crusades of the nineteen thirties,
fifties, and sixties. It is worth noting that in Hightown
the Christian Americans who fought hardest to keep
Christmas in the public schools had only the most fragile
bonds with organized religion, Protestant, Roman Catholic, or Jewish.

Chapter IV

Church and State in Christian History

AMERICAN THINKING ON CHURCH AND STATE WAS formed by a stream of history rising in the Middle Ages, flowing through John Calvin to English and American Puritanism, then by way of the American Revolution into the nineteenth-century America with its new, large minorities completely untouched by the Reformation and Puritan movements. At the beginning of this history, church and state were closely harmonized; at its outcome in America, they had been separated.

THE UNITY OF CHURCH AND STATE

Biblically oriented Christians, like Jews, have always believed that the whole world belongs to God. They have never believed that there are two sorts of life, one belonging to God, the other to man. But they have expressed this conviction in different ways of relating church and state.

The Middle Ages (600–1500) embraced a considerable range of thought on church and state, and it is important to recognize that for all the unity of European society then, there was still great variety. Yet medieval theologians—political thinkers were theologians—agreed that the spiritual aspect of life was fundamental and unalterable and must embrace and rule all that changes. The supremacy of the church in the Middle Ages arose from its monopoly of God's gifts of grace, without which men could not be delivered from sin and hell. The state was not believed to be altogether cut off from God; still, any state that would serve God's purposes must look to the church for both guidance and authority.

To some medieval thinkers, this meant that the pope was the supreme interpreter of all law in church and civil life. Kingship itself was constituted by the church, they argued. Kings were crowned by popes to signify that they exercised their office as agents of God under the authority and direction of the pope. On this theory kings did not possess royal authority solely because they had lawfully succeeded to the throne but because, having lawfully become kings, the church established their right to exercise civil authority.

It is important to draw a line between the view that the spiritual realm is in some sense superior to the temporal and the view that the church exercises political authority over the state. In the latter scheme, the church has the right to direct the affairs of civil society through kings and other magistrates.

John Calvin held to the first of these but not the second. He denied that the clergy should control civil power or direct kings, but he strongly affirmed that rulers and the whole public needed the guidance of the church. In his model town of Geneva, Switzerland, Calvin put the entire teaching responsibility into the hands of the church and clergy—not just the teaching of religion but also the moral guidance of politics and family life. Ministers constantly spoke on public questions.

As for the state, Calvin believed that kings and other civil officials receive their authority directly from God, not by way of the church. To be sure, good Calvinist magistrates listened to the teaching of their churches!

While their office did not depend on the church, their understanding of how to run it certainly did. Furthermore, the laws of the Calvinist state were the very laws of God, and they therefore clearly protected a Calvinist church. Offenses against the church were punishable by civil laws. In these regards, Calvin remained medieval. Still, in Calvin's view no king was a church agent for ruling the people; he was God's own agent for civil affairs. Here was a critically important difference from the medieval order.

Calvin made a second important change in an ancient view of the state. Why should there be any state at all? After all, God established none in the Garden of Eden! Had he not resisted the Hebrew people when they demanded a king? The usual answer was that sin threw men into conflict with one another and the state was a device to keep sin from bringing mankind to wreck. Without it, wicked men would have everything their own way. The state was a sort of negative necessity.

Calvin agreed that an important function of the state was to check criminals and political aggressors, but he added the idea, not original with him, that God created the state to be an agent of positive good. Calvin was by no means an advocate of the modern welfare state; the whole conception of the modern state was foreign to him. But neither was he a "less government the better" man. Calvin even called the civil magistrates "ministers of God." In his rather large book that was about as far as you could go.

What did Calvin do to separate church and state?

Geneva was a halfway step from medievalism to the modern world. Calvin separated church authority from state authority. The church's sphere is spiritual, he said, the state's temporal. The church can excommunicate a sinner (forbid him to take Communion) but not imprison him; the state may imprison a criminal but not excommunicate him. Both church and state are established by God; each has its own sphere; the church does not establish or formally confirm the state on God's behalf. Calvin taught that a king was answerable only to God for his misdeeds as a ruler, although if he were a church member he must confess his sin exactly like other Christians. It would be a foolish king indeed who would imagine that he could know all that God wanted him to know without listening to church teaching. But such foolish kings were still kings. To be sure, it was the duty of the nobility and lower officers in government to restrain and, within the bounds of their offices, to frustrate a bad king's evil designs. But this was not the same as outright rebellion. In Calvin's opinion, even a government that persecuted the church remained a true state if it continued to discharge the duties of a state in some substantial way. He taught that a persecuted church should resort to "prayers and tears," not popular rebellion and certainly not any political effort by the church, to unseat the king in favor of someone selected by the clergy.

The Separateness of Church and State

Religious toleration was unheard of in Geneva. Its laws required every citizen to accept church instruction and forbade anyone to dispute the Reformed faith or attack the clergy. For his assault on Christian doctrine and unconcealed bitterness toward Calvin, Michael Servetus, an early Unitarian, was burned at the stake by order of a Genevan government heavily influenced by the ministers. Geneva guaranteed Reformed religion, not religious freedom.

After 1560 it became increasingly difficult throughout Europe to maintain nationwide agreement on religious belief. In France, a series of unbelievably cruel wars ended in 1598 with a restless truce between Roman Catholics and Protestants; about 1645 persecution of Protestants was resumed, and in 1685 their liberties were formally revoked. An estimated two hundred thousand fled into exile, impoverishing French industry, wounding the public spirit, and delivering the nation into a glittering tyranny that ended at the guillotine in 1793.

In England matters took a different course. Religious diversity flourished there even more than in France. After civil war the English took a more practical course: an Act of Toleration in 1689 forbade persecution of Englishmen for religious opinion and granted the right to churches and sects to live unmolested by the government at the side of the established church of England.

No one liked toleration. Many Puritans believed that it had ruined true religion and a dedicated handful attempted to set up in Massachusetts a commonwealth like Geneva. But it did not work. First Roger Williams left, proclaiming the right of individuals to worship as they wished and attacking the pretensions of a government that presumed to operate solely according to the laws of God.

Virginia attempted to curb the growth of non-Episcopal groups even after 1689, but Samuel Davies, a Presbyterian missionary, doggedly fought the colonial government. Just before the Revolution, Jefferson and Madison, supported by Baptists and Presbyterians, wrote separation of church and state into the Virginia constitution.

New York's governor, Lord Cornbury, jailed Francis Makemie, a Presbyterian preacher, for conducting worship without his permission; but Makemie's appeal was successful, and Cornbury was recalled to England in disgrace.

All efforts to unite church and state by law in North America failed. Partly this was because men like Roger Williams and William Penn regarded religious liberty as a positive value; but the more general reason was that the colonists simply could not agree on the correct form of Christianity. The alternative to separation of church and state was civil strife and the degradation of religion itself.

We have now come to the point in American history when the First Amendment was drafted. Some Americans in the 1780's believed that it did not separate church and state rigidly enough. While Virginia was discussing the Constitution, eight of its Senators wrote: "[The Amendment] recommended by Congress does not prohibit the rights of conscience from being violated or infringed; and although it goes to restrain Congress from passing laws establishing any national religion, they might, notwithstanding, levy taxes to any amount for the support of religion or its preachers." That last point had been hotly contested in Virginia.

The First Amendment was not radical. Not only was Congress left free to levy taxes for church support; the Amendment did nothing to prevent state governments from legalizing a chosen church within their own boundaries. (That Constitutional prohibition came only with the Fourteenth Amendment in 1868.) Presbyterians were very numerous in Pennsylvania in 1780, and there was some public fear that they would seek favors for their church. The ruling body of Presbyterianism replied in 1783: "The Synod do solemnly and publicly declare that they ever have and still do renounce and abhor the principles of intolerance, and we do believe that every peaceable member of civil society ought to be protected in the full and free exercise of his religion."

In 1788 the Presbyterians confirmed this position in the Constitution of their new General Assembly, the successor body to the synod of the above statement. " 'God alone is Lord of the conscience and hath left it free from the doctrines and commandments of men which are in anything contrary to his Word, or beside it, in matters of faith and worship.' Therefore [Presbyterians] consider the rights of private judgment, in all matters that respect religion, as universal and unalienable; they do not even wish to see any religious constitution aided by the civil power, further than may be necessary for protection and security and at the same time, be equal and common to others."

With Justice Douglas and others, Presbyterians see no reason why policemen should not protect their children on the way to church; but the same public services must be available to all, and such services are as far as government ought to go in "aiding" churches.

The old theocratic notions lasted a little longer in New England. But Connecticut got rid of its state church in 1819; Massachusetts, in 1833. That was the end of state religion in the United States. Since 1868 it has been unconstitutional for *any* American governmental body to enact laws either favoring or constraining any practice of religion that is consistent with civil order.

SEPARATION OR ISOLATION?

There have always been Americans who have called for the withdrawal of religious people from worldly society. The Amish of Pennsylvania are perhaps the best known. Plain black clothing instead of modern styles; buggies instead of cars; refusal of military service; hard work with little pleasure; stay-at-home living instead of gadding around—to them, religion demands separation not only from the state but from the world.

The religious impulse of retreat from the temptations of life has never been limited to the Amish or even to the sects. In the second quarter of the nineteenth century the mood of withdrawal ran very strong among American Calvinists, who had traditionally made decided efforts to influence public affairs. But they had been deeply shocked by events between the Revolutionary War and the 1830's.

Tom Paine, the popular Revolutionary philosopher, had argued that the basis of the new nation was man's reason, not the will of God. The new doctrines of political liberty seemed to troubled Calvinists to owe more to Voltaire and Montesquieu than to Paul and John Calvin. The Constitutional guarantees of religious liberty were welcome to Presbyterians—but not the philosophy of Thomas Jefferson, who was overwhelmingly opposed by the Calvinist clergy in the election of 1800.

The outbreak of slavery controversy after 1830 dealt a paralyzing blow to Calvinist concern for public affairs. Southern Presbyterians insisted that slavery was a political, not a moral, question. Northerners saw that if slavery dispute should ever intrude on the churches, they would be divided. There was wide agreement both north and south that the debate on slavery should be separated from religion. Even this point of view commanded no consensus, however, and division descended relentlessly on the American churches.

Partly because so many churches split over politics, by 1840 the notion that a line should be drawn between all public affairs and spiritual religion was widespread among American Christians. A mood of withdrawal was in the air. Where Presbyterians had once worked in legislatures and executive offices to change the country, they now retired to their closets for prayer.

The era of withdrawal did not end quickly—many members of large modern denominations still consider religion a purely private matter—but the wind changed about 1870. Shortly after the end of the Civil War, industrial development spurted forward, particularly in the northeastern quarter of the nation. Its side effects shocked and aroused the Christian conscience. Slums and poverty had always existed in the cities of America, but now the swift expansion of industry created great concentrations of workers around factories. Newly arrived immigrants, often disoriented, were at the mercy of unemployment and corrupt political machines.

North America was founded by immigrants, but the arrival of massive minority groups that knew nothing of the Puritan tradition was another matter. The Irish, solidly Roman Catholic, came by the hundred thousands after 1830 and settled in urban ghettos. The slaves had followed a religion of mixed paganism and lay Christianity but until their emancipation were looked on rather as property than persons. After their liberation they began to move to the cities.

Between 1890 and 1920, when immigration was drastically curbed, the industrial cities of the nation received wave upon wave of peoples who erected their own churches, founded their own social clubs, and often lived cheek by jowl. By 1870, the country was no longer Protestant; by 1910, the hinge of its economic life was the factory, not the farm.

Just as 1770 marked the beginning of a new century in the political life of our country, 1870 opened a new chapter in the social awareness of the American churches. Within forty years all the major churches of the country had recognized that the mood of withdrawal was unfit for the new times. Separation of church and state was indispensable, but the continued isolation of the churches from the lives of people struggling for existence in industrial society would be fatal to religion.

Christians pondered what they should do. Should churches speak out about child labor? Should they do something about drunkenness? Political corruption? Strikes? Were these any concern of churches as such?

While considerable numbers still doubted whether religion belonged in factories, saloons, and legislative halls, a significant clerical leadership answered these questions with an unmistakable Yes. But *how* the churches should act was not so clear. Was the church going to intervene in affairs of state?

For many centuries, churches had relieved human misery by acts of charity. The baffling new feature of the industrial age was that charity could not rebuild cities, annul obsolete laws, or regulate labor practices. These goals could be achieved only by new legislation. Should church influence be brought to bear on lawmaking? Would this breach the precious wall separating church and state? If the church should advocate relief of social suffering by law, could this be done without infringing church-state separation?

By 1910 the leading American churches were reasonably sure that it was morally obligatory for them to seek justice for workers who could not obtain a fair share of the product of their labor. Churchmen knew that this must be accomplished by law. They affirmed that there must be no mixing of institutional church power with government power but demanded strong representations of Christian opinion by churchmen and others of similar views to legislators and public executives. American Protestant leadership was once again taking responsibility for the whole life of the society.

Chapter V

Brief Intermission — Where We Have Been and Where We Are Going

THUS FAR IN THIS STUDY WE HAVE DESCRIBED HIGH-town, U.S.A., an American community that was shocked to find itself inflamed by a fear-ridden dispute on a common American practice: Christmas celebrations in the public schools. We have analyzed the solution worked out by Hightown, and we have described the understanding of church and state that exists in Hightown, U.S.A., and then discussed the national viewpoint, seen mainly in Supreme Court decisions and the opinions of dissenting judges. We have sampled various Christian views of church-state relations, ranging from the Middle Ages to several sorts of separation of church and state practiced since the Reformation.

What we have not yet done is to state what American Protestants, Roman Catholics, Jews, and the religiously uncommitted *now* believe about church-state relations.

There are difficulties here. First, the major American subcommunities have by no means achieved internal agreement on church-state relations. Second, what these four sorts of Americans think about the relation of church and state occasionally appears in books and articles but what they *do* about it is vastly more important. What they do, they always do in connection with particular disputes. Still, we can list the disputed church-state issues without too much trouble, so here is a list of the favorite American battlefields on the frontier of church-state relations.

ISSUES HINGING ON THE USE OF TAX FUNDS

Religious observances in the public schools. This is a tax issue because the buildings, supplies, and instruction are purchased from tax funds.

The appropriation of tax funds to church-related schools. Discussion of this problem generally distinguishes primary and secondary schools from colleges, universities, and graduate and professional schools. While some questions are raised about tax aid to higher education, a very large number of Americans doubt that state funds may be constitutionally used to subsidize primary and secondary church schools. There is also a question of state aid to private *non*church affiliated schools, but this does not raise the church-state issue itself.

The appropriation of tax funds for aid to church-related hospitals, clinics, health education centers, and welfare institutions. This is closely related to the question of tax aid to church-related schools.

The birth control debate. There are two particular sides of this issue under discussion: (1) Whether tax funds, partly paid by Roman Catholics, should be spent to sponsor foreign aid programs that include education and advice in the use of chemical and mechanical methods of preventing conception (as a means of population control). (2) Whether in public institutions, supported by taxes partly paid by Roman Catholics, birth control advice and related medical services should be offered.

The exemption of church properties from local real estate taxes. This raises the question whether churches should enjoy fire and police protection and other public services at the expense of the community at large, which generally includes many who do not share the religion of the church benefited.

The maintenance of military chaplains at public expense.

PREFERENTIAL TREATMENT, CIVIL RIGHTS, AND RELIGIOUS FREEDOM

The exemption of candidates for the ministry, priesthood, and rabbinate from military service. Why should these students not share the national burden of military service with all others?

Sunday closing laws. While supported by many as a defense of laboring people from prolonged working hours, by social agencies as useful for the defense of family life, and by many people for a variety of reasons, Sunday closing laws bear heavily on those who for religious reasons close their businesses on Saturday but cannot open them on Sunday because the Christian day of worship is restricted by law.

The evaluation of the fitness of candidates for public office on the basis of religious affiliation.

Censorship by public or semipublic agencies (of printed materials, motion pictures, and other media) which favors the religious scruples of one religious group above another, or of religion above nonreligious opinion, or is critical of religious belief and religious institutions.

The effect of religious attitudes and precedents on laws and the administration of laws governing marriage and divorce and the adoption of children.

Exemption of conscientious objectors from military service who profess religious motives.

While this list of disputed points by no means covers all the ways in which the church-state issue can crop up in American political life, a very good understanding of church-state relations is possible to a person who has pondered them in the perspectives which these disputes open to us.

Another preliminary note. There is no "Protestant position" on church-state relations and there never will be, not because Protestants find it hard to agree among themselves—which they do—so much as because the relationship between religious minorities and the whole American social system is constantly changing. Each change brings a new response from Protestants.

The same is true of Roman Catholics and Jews, although in a somewhat more limited degree. It is more limited for Roman Catholics because the Roman Catholic Church is organized to make decisions and ascertain its position more explicitly on moral issues, while Protestants are not. It is more limited for Jews because the Jewish community is profoundly united in its concern for a political order radically dedicated to civil and religious liberty. Yet the Roman Catholic Church permits thorough debate of all issues that do not question doctrines on which that church has in some official way agreed—and church-state relations are not among the already decided positions.

Nonreligious Americans are perhaps the least united by community ties; they agree issue by issue and re-form their ranks as the battle changes.

While it is impossible to state the "Protestant position" in church and state or any other major point, the distinctness of Protestants in relation to the other main American groups stands out as strongly in church-state matters as on any other. Given the diversity of these groups, it is practicable to attempt to state at least the angles of vision from which American groups examine the issue of church-state relations in their country.

One more preliminary problem. What about the lunatic fringe? It is an embarrassing fact that a number of Protestant church members, some of them clergymen, are out-and-out bigots: publishers of hate propaganda, local demagogues, political irresponsibles. The Roman Catholic Church has been deeply embarrassed from time to time by certain figures of its own: Father Coughlin and the late Senator Joseph McCarthy, for example. The presence of extremists within the membership of the churches makes it impossible to disavow them altogether; yet it is neither fair nor productive of understanding to treat these radicals as spokesmen of their groups.

It is a real question whether the lunatic fringe of the churches is seriously affected by religious beliefs. A decision has to be made. In the discussion that follows, we will not treat the lunatic fringe as an integral part of American church life.

It may seem arbitrary to say that the sectarian clergyman who circulates hate propaganda is not really a Protestant; but it is at least fair to exclude him if we also exonerate the Roman Catholic Church of responsibility for its own agitators. Furthermore, it is possible to demonstrate that the utterances and actions of such people have relatively little to do with the theological beliefs and historical attitudes of the churches in which they maintain membership. Their acts arise from the dominion of fear. Is it not reasonable to argue that persons who have never experienced the release from fear and prejudice that is one of the first benefits of religious faith ought to be excluded from consideration when we speak of Protestant and Roman Catholic approaches to church-state relations? Bigotry is one of the gravest problems of church-state relations in American democracy, but little is gained by taxing Protestants at large with fostering prejudice or blaming the Roman Catholic Church for the erratic conduct of a handful of priests and laymen.

Chapter VI

Protestant Views of Church and State

PROTESTANTS ARE SOLID FOR SEPARATION OF CHURCH and state in much the same way they are solid for God, home, and country. The real question is: What does separation of church and state mean to them when it touches the specific questions we have listed?

Critics of Protestants sometimes point out that they are for separation of church and state until they get caught in the separator themselves. They are for separation, all right—but what is so bad about reading the New Testament to first-graders? Reservations are so abundant in the minds of some Protestants that Roman Catholics sometimes wryly refer to the "Protestant public-school system." There is some justice in the remark.

How can the attitudes of the widely different kinds of Protestants be pulled together into a general description of the Protestant approach to church and state?

At least one statement is possible: Almost all Protestants agree with Justice William Douglas that "we are a religious people." The great majority are therefore moderate separationists; they do not want complete separation of church and state.

This leads to a second generalization: Protestants are pragmatic rather than doctrinaire in their understanding of church-state relations. Once they have accepted the need for change, they ask: What adjustment can and ought to be made? They usually do not start by asking: What does the principle of separation of church and state require?

The reason for this may be stated as a third generalization. Protestants are usually friendly to existing custom and would rather modify it than write a new plan for the life of the community. Most American communities were (many still are) predominantly Protestant when social change began, as with Hightown. Justified or not, Protestants move slowly in matters of community changes.

Conservative, pragmatic, and sometimes inconsistent, Protestants are also completely earnest about the separation of church and state. There are strong historical reasons for this. The prolonged contest in colonial Virginia for freedom from religious taxes, universal Protestant support for the First Amendment, suspicion of all philosophical approaches to politics, continuing fear among even the best informed and most balanced Protestant thinkers that the Roman Catholic Church is not fundamentally committed to the separation of church and state, and the feeling that the health of religion itself is threatened by the intermixing of religion with public law solidify the Protestant community in support of separation of church and state as the best safeguard for religious liberty. The degree of agreement among Protestants is altogether remarkable, considering the large number of Protestant bodies in the United States and their diffuse organization. The problem of Protestants is not the temptation to abandon the principle of separation of church and state, despite their reluctance to push it to any great length, but rather a widespread refusal to accept a reasonable application of it in a nation no longer mostly Protestant.

Let us attempt to discover the Protestant approach to church-state relations by stating a set of contrasts between Roman Catholics, Protestants, and strong separationists on the disputed issue of birth control. We must note that the Protestant community has only begun to examine this issue. The following discussion, therefore, is rooted in historic Protestant positions and does not pretend to state any contemporary agreement.

Roman Catholics believe that birth control is primarily a religious and moral issue falling clearly within the jurisdiction of church authority and is only secondarily, if at all, a political question. Secondly, they believe that procreation is the primary purpose of sexual union and that God provides through family, church, and state the means for sustaining all who are born into the world; and thirdly, they believe that simply because the current excess of population over food supply in some areas of the world has made birth control a political issue, government has no right to support education in the use of devices to prevent conception. Yet the Roman Catholic Church believes that laws may be passed restricting medical counsel and sale of birth control devices.

Most Protestants believe that birth control is a religious, moral, and political issue with which the whole public (and therefore the state) is deeply involved. Secondly, they hold that the purpose of sexual union is the realization of the richest possible union of one man and one woman in marriage, which includes the bearing and rearing of children; and thirdly, consistent with the religious and moral sentiment of the people as a whole, the state may support voluntary birth control education programs, provided the religious and moral convictions of medical and administrative personnel are in no way violated.

Can we detect within the Protestant approach to birth control a Protestant approach to church-state relations?

It should first be noted that in discussing birth control, church-state relations has subtly become a problem of the relation of religion and morals to political action. It is certainly possible to keep institutional churches reasonably free of legal entanglement with government, but is it possible to separate religion and morals from politics?

Political decisions almost always have a moral side. A government that neglects justice is not a true state—and justice is a matter of morals. If politics were to be separated from religion, religion would have to be separated from morals! Neither Roman Catholic, Protestant, nor Jew will consent to such separation. It would mean the reduction of religion to mysticism and ritual, deprivation of its right to act, and proclamation of its irrelevance to man's social existence.

The Protestant approach attempts to separate neither religion from morals nor morals from politics. It nevertheless insists on reasonable and consistent separation of church and state. To press the logic of separation to its extreme would demand the rupture of politics and morals. That was precisely what Hitler did: for him, politics simply absorbed and supplanted morals. It is possible, of course, to hand over morals to politics and isolate religion. A few nonreligious separationists manage this to their own satisfaction, but American Christians and Jews will have none of it and that makes it a politically useless choice.

The Roman Catholic position, on the other hand, accuses the state of acting immorally when it encourages or permits birth control education in any of its institutions or programs. Roman Catholics do not separate religion from morals or either of these from politics. The result is a demand that the state should never interfere with the freedom of the Roman Catholic to live in conformity with the teaching of his church.

GOD, CHURCH, AND STATE

At this point there appears a fundamental theoretical difference between the Roman Catholic view of the state and the Protestant view. These agree that God is supreme over both church and state. But Roman Catholic theology affirms that the concern of God with man is expressed primarily and authoritatively through the church, which is above all a spiritual body; that the sphere of the state is the temporal life of man; and that the church possesses a moral authority superior to the state, the family, and all other forms of human life.

The terms "spiritual" and "temporal" have become vague in modern usage, but they have been lavishly used by both Roman Catholic and Protestant thinkers throughout Christian history. In historic use, "spiritual" has meant at least three things: all that is eternal and unchanging (the temporal not only changes but eventually passes away altogether) second, the inward life of man—his conscience, motives, and attitudes; third, a strictly theological usage: everything that occurs by the power of the Holy Spirit, the third person of the Christian Trinity. Both Roman Catholic and Protestant believe that an all-important tie exists between God and man's inner life of conscience. Both hold that it is unlawful for governments to seek to bind consciences on the ground that this would be an intrusion on the spiritual. Conscience is the court of man's experience where the eternal is heard. Conscience is the "spiritual" side of man.

In modern times it is recognized that the inner life of man cannot be so readily separated from his conduct. Luther took the older view: No matter what oppressions a Christian might suffer, his inward freedom could never be taken from him. Since Luther's time, the brainwashers have learned how to destroy man's inward freedom and the advertisers have found ways to implant inward compulsions. Men today are forced by psychological pressures to act contrary to their reasoned convictions and, artificially motivated, to do things contrary to their free choice. The "spiritual" is very much a part of the life of man in the flesh and the world. Furthermore, it is now recognized that conscience may be formed, even dominated, by environment. Conscience is at least as much affected by the temporal as the eternal. If a man's spiritual life is to be benefited, his social circumstances must be taken into account. When a man's circumstances change, his motives, feelings, and even his conscience are affected.

This has importance for the church. In a day when theology believed that no change of outward condition—employment, law, or disease—could infringe freedom of conscience, the church could argue that the gospel was medicine for the soul and had little to do with society and government. But now the church must speak to all the conditions—social, psychological, legal—that so profoundly affect the inward freedom of man. An obvious example is religious toleration: legal restrictions on worship and religious education inhibit the spiritual development of a citizen. Churches must, therefore, act concretely in public affairs to safeguard the freedom of all citizens.

Roman Catholic, Lutheran, and other theologies, however, continue to use the terms "spiritual" and "temporal." Roman Catholic theology affirms that the spiritual is superior to the temporal and the church is superior to the state. Modern Protestant theology, by contrast, refuses to hold the physical and political life of man in lower esteem than the religious life. For the Protestant, the coming of Christ in a human body to assume his place in human society lent eternal significance to man's temporal experience and all the institutions of time.

In this perspective it can be acknowledged that the state deals in the "spiritual" as much as the church deals in the "temporal." Courts, for example, attempt to determine degrees of guilt by considering such "spiritual" factors as motivation, premeditation, and mental state. It is all but impossible to distinguish church and state along the traditional lines of the spiritual and the temporal.

Here we encounter the problem of the "moral." Morality is related to both the inward life of man and what he does. All Biblically oriented Christians and Jews believe that life is moral. But the Roman Catholic affirms that morality belongs to the realm of the spiritual. The arbitration of moral questions, therefore, belongs primarily to the church in Roman Catholic thought. Most Protestants believe that problems of public morals must be solved in the context of the state. This does not mean that there are two moralities, one of the church, another of the state. Morality is one, and all morality is subject to God's law. It does mean that the church is not and may not regard itself as better qualified than the state to determine morals for the whole people. That task God has laid on the state. The state exists in obedience to a special command of God relating to civil government; this command is different from God's command to the church, although church and state exist in definite relationships. God has provided that the state shall be his primary servant in civil matters; and he further provides in his mercy that states actually can be relatively just in their administration of temporal power. Christians ought therefore be concerned that states be just to all, not that they bend their laws to favor special religious or other partisan interests. God's will for the state is not only distinct from his will for the church; state authority is broader in its own way than the authority wielded by any actual church on earth.

Protestants hold that the state ought to listen carefully to all the admonitions that may be addressed to it by any church as by all other responsible voices. Furthermore, if a state should become unjust by forcing Christians to make a clear choice between God and government, they would choose God. But when such conflicts arise, the church does not assert a natively superior moral insight into public questions. The church indicts bad government for failure to know justice and act on it, something that a state in its own proper character is both able and required to do. Even when Christian citizens join in rebellion against a hopelessly corrupt government, they do not pretend that the church as such is a judge over the state; they simply claim that a government has failed so totally that a true state is no longer enshrined by it. In Protestant thinking, respect for the state arises not out of an ecclesiastical imprimatur but in the fact that God himself has instituted the state and laid it on the consciences of his people to support it and protect it from destruction. The state does not make its own morals; exactly like churches, governments are bound to live by the laws of God. When churches point this out, they still make no claim to be morally superior to the state.

This throws interesting light on the Roman Catholic critique of public programs of birth control education. Protestants, too, frequently disagree with their government's moral reasoning and may even agree wholeheartedly with Roman Catholic criticism of birth control. But Protestant disagreement with government contains no unvoiced assumption of the general authority of church over state in moral matters. The state takes full responsibility before God for its decisions. When it is criticized by the church it is not being arraigned before a higher moral tribunal. The church does have something that even the best state does not have: The church is gifted with the knowledge of the gospel and has a duty of witness which is unique to it. This should render Christian men sensitive to the gravity of the law and the holiness of God, but it imparts no knowledge of law beyond what God has conferred on the state. The state stands in the same court of judgment where the church stands, before the throne of God.

To some people this may seem a very theoretical difference but to the Roman Catholic administrator of a tax-supported clinic where birth control information is disseminated it is far from theoretical. He has an obligation to the moral teachings of his church; with him this is a matter of conscience. He is also morally obligated to the policies of his government. If his church is superior to the state in moral matters, it is quite clear that he cannot obey his superiors in government. He sins when he disobeys the higher authority. If government has the right to make judgments in its own sphere (and is, on balance, a just and true government) the Catholic civil servant is not only free to act on its directives but morally obligated to disseminate birth control information in the face of his church's opinion. He may personally disagree with his government's policy and protest it as a citizen, but he does not commit sin in performing his duty. In the Protestant view, he sins if he fails to serve a just government according to its own laws. What a public servant may not do is to administer a civil position in conformity with ecclesiastical teachings that conflict with public policy.

But what about war? At certain times, war *is* public policy. The state ought not (though in its extremity it perhaps has the right to) compel any citizen to perform or accept services morally abhorrent to him. On this ground, conscientious objectors to war are not compelled to study the arts of killing. Roman Catholic administrators, like conscientious objectors, may serve government well in positions where conscience does not clash with public policy.

While conscientious objectors are excused from military service (or at least line duties) they are not excused from paying taxes to buy the machines of war. There government draws the line. So also with tax support of public birth control clinics: Roman Catholics ought not be compelled to administer them nor accept their services, but they cannot be excused from supporting them through equitable taxation. Millions of Americans pay taxes that are spent on causes which they disapprove. When in public matters a conflict occurs between personal conviction and public necessity, adjustment is often possible, but public necessity prevails. As with national defense, so with population control.

Let us summarize our conclusions about the Protestant approach to church-state relations so far as they can be extracted from Protestant thought on birth control education.

1. The state is inevitably involved with moral issues.

2. To the state belongs both the right and the responsibility of deciding moral issues that touch the public interest. Having received its right from God, the state is accountable only to him for its laws and rulings, not to any church.

3. Morals always ought to be intimately conjoined with religion.

4. Absolute separation of religion from politics is therefore impossible and undesirable.

5. Total separation between church and state is likewise both impossible and undesirable.

6. It is both possible and necessary, however, to maintain general separation of institutional churches and sectarian practices on the one hand from all organs of civil authority on the other, through a series of practical judgments. Such judgments will be made with equal regard to the defense of religious liberty and the right of the state to freedom in its own sphere.

7. The state is obligated to vindicate the freedom of the consciences of all its citizens as fully as possible, particularly when they have deep-seated moral reservations about public programs.

8. Churches are within their rights in discussing public moral issues, assisting their members to relate them-

selves responsibly to laws and policies they disapprove, actively encouraging their members to seek changes in laws by democratic methods, and urging their moral convictions on the whole public.

9. Churches may claim freedom of conscience and the rights of religious liberty but not special favor for themselves or their members.

10. Churches may press for specific measures that they deem necessary to the public welfare, but they ought not commit themselves permanently to a fixed set of partisan concerns.

11. As an ultimate guarantee of their liberty, citizens possess an innate right to refuse to support the state, even to the point of open rebellion against a government that has fallen into corruption.

Chapter VII

Roman Catholic Views of Church and State

IN FORMULATING THEIR VIEWS ON CHURCH-STATE issues, Roman Catholic thinkers usually work from well-defined principles. The more practical approach of Protestants does not mean that they are unconcerned about basic principles, nor is Roman Catholic thought necessarily doctrinaire. Precisely how this works can be seen in the disputed issue of tax support for church-related schools.

Roman Catholics believe that (1) a sound society is founded upon laws which God himself has implanted in the minds of men, laws which are best understood in association with Roman Catholic religious teaching; (2) among these laws is "distributive justice" (explained on page 62); (3) due regard for distributive justice is just as essential to a healthy democracy as the First Amendment, and these are not in contradiction; and therefore (4) both natural law and the American Constitution are best served by granting tax assistance to church-related schools.

Roman Catholic thought depends on the conception of natural law, of which distributive justice is a part. Here we will outline natural law and state some alternative views.

NATURAL LAW

How does a thinking man decide what he will do when faced with an unfamiliar situation?

Partly, of course, he will be guided by previous experience in similar circumstances. The past has its lessons. But analysis of experience sometimes yields no sure guidelines; a situation may be radically different; a decision may have such great significance that men are impelled to seek more secure foundations for decision than human experience. At such times they appeal from history and experience to philosophy and theology. History changes; the principles revealed by philosophy and theology, they believe, are everywhere true and unchanging.

This is the judgment of thinkers who speak of natural law. What men do, they argue, is a matter for historians and sociologists to describe; what they ought to do can be discovered only by direct knowledge of fundamental moral principles.

What are the principles that affect men's lives in matters civil and religious? Philosophers and theologians of many schools of thought agree that man is a particular sort of being who lives by rules that differ from the rules that govern the behavior of stars, porpoises, or palm trees. One faculty in particular marks man off from other beings: his reason. These philosophers and theologians give the name "natural law" to the body of principle that sets limits to the way men behave and teaches how they ought to behave. Men may violate natural law, but they do so at mortal risk. If they would know and do good, they must learn the law, conform to it, and enforce it on all who would abuse it. Natural law governs both solitary and social conduct. Law is inherent in society, just as law is innate to rational individuals.

Natural law exists within men in the form of reason,

say these thinkers; and it exists outside them in the form
of a rational order of nature. Order in man's reason appears in consistent and logical thought. In nature, it
appears as regular growth, self-preservation, and adapta-
tion to change. Advocates of natural law hold that man's
inner reason and the laws of nature outside him are in
agreement and that successful life in family, church, and
state depends on man's grasp of natural law and obedience to it.

Are there any other answers to the question of the
ground and order on which man's life rests?

Positive Law: Ethical Relativism

There are two main alternatives to natural law theory:
one advocated by opponents of older philosophical solu-
tions and the other, surprisingly, by some Protestant theologians.

The nonreligious critic of natural law points out that
no one can prove that it actually exists and that as useful
as reason undoubtedly is, it is far from agreeing with
itself at all times and among all men. Take family life,
for example. Proponents of natural law from Aristotle to
modern Roman Catholicism state that the family is a
universal institution among men and can be accounted
for only by a fundamental law in man's nature. To this
the critic replies: Does not family life have many forms,
depending on the practical needs of people? Cannot the
universal occurrence of political organization of some kind
be explained by the obvious fact that without it, people
would exterminate one another? Why add a superfluous
theory about "the nature of things" to the observable facts?

The truth is, argue these practical minds, that natural
law is not the root of the facts; it is a product of culture.
The modern family and state have been built piece by
piece out of accumulating experience. What they are in

essence is an empty question; they are just what history has made them, no more and no less. Law, therefore, is composed one step at a time. What the law should be must be decided on practical grounds as the future unfolds. The only valid rule is simply what serves best. By their own decisions, men *posit* law and that is its whole substance.

We will not pause to argue this position. What do theological critics of natural law say?

REVEALED LAW

It was all very well for Aristotle to construct a theory of natural law, reply certain modern theologians, but Christians have no business with it at all. The first fact for man is not the laws of reason and nature but God. The question of law ought to be a question about God. Furthermore, it is not a question about the "nature" of God but simply an inquiry about what God has done. If God has done something, presumably man will find truth there: the truth about himself, the world, and morals. As a matter of fact, God has done something: he sent his own Son, Jesus Christ, into the world after a long period of preparation. (Because of their emphasis on Christ these critics may be called Christologists.) Christians have reflected at length on the meaning of this act of God. Is it not the first duty of Christians to inquire not about the natural law but after the divine law revealed in Christ? And when they do this, may they not find it unnecessary or even misleading to ask questions about another sort of law besides the divine law?

The actual fact is that Christian theology has held both theories, natural law and revealed law. For most of its history the church has believed that there is both a law of God and a law of nature, and that nature is subject to God and should obey him because it is his creation.

What is wrong with this double theory? Does it do an injustice to God?

Theological critics of natural law claim, in the first place, that the theory separates man from God improperly. A Roman Catholic may say: Natural law is what man's reason knows without divine aid; divine law is what can be known only when God reveals it. Some Protestants argue that man is responsible to natural law because all men, even without Jesus Christ, can know that law; but no one is responsible to the divine law except Christians, since only they know Christ.

There are other ways of separating the realm of nature from the realm of God. What is wrong with all such theories, argue the Christologists, is that in one way or another they all set the ability and will of man over against the freedom and will of God. They suggest that man, without the assistance of revelation, can in some degree please God; but was not the fundamental reason for the coming of Christ precisely man's total inability to know and do the will of God? When God made man a free being, he made him responsible to himself; he did not make man the prince of some realm removed from God's authority. Nor did God put within the reach of men the possibility of perfect goodness in some way dissociated from himself. When man (Adam is his symbol) got confused about this, he "fell"; i.e., became the slave of a deathly misunderstanding and followed the wrong way ever after. It is in restoration to actual fellowship with God that man's future lies; not in the perfecting of any innate moral capacities of his own.

The critical need of man, Christologists argue, is to heal this breach with God, and by this to recover his native powers. This is why Christ was sent. He effected man's reconciliation with God. He reconstituted the fellowship with God on which every human possibility depends. The work of Christ does not set man back on the path toward moral self-sufficiency but on the path to God himself. Therefore when we speak of law we *must* speak of divine law as the all-encompassing order and rule of man's life. It is not man's capacity for moral idealism but God's revelation of himself in Christ, the perfect man, to which we must turn if we would know how to live.

These three main points of view about the ground of human experience cannot be easily combined. While neither the natural-law theorists nor the Christologists ignore the practical political experience of the nations, they do reject the claim of proponents of positive law that there is no underlying order at all but only many layers of human tradition deposited by what has happened.

The natural law theorist, although far from denying the Kingship of Christ, still affirms that man's life is best understood with the help of some notion of natural law. To him, divine law must have its counterpart in man and nature. Christologists are the most adamant of all: either Christ is Lord or he is not—a choice must be made. They demand that the notion of natural law be abandoned. They absolutely reject the idea that human experience, no matter how prolonged or how wisely pondered, can be the rule of man's life.

ROMAN CATHOLICS, NATURAL LAW, AND THE SCHOOL QUESTION

Just how does the theory of natural law affect Roman Catholic thought on the question of tax aid to church-related schools? The claim of the Roman Catholic Church on tax support for parochial schools (primary and secondary schools affiliated with *any* church body) rests on the principle of distributive justice which "requires that those who stand equal before a law and its defined purpose shall be equal in relation to such burdens and benefits as that law entails."

Here is the way the Rev. William Gorman, a Roman Catholic writer, argues for tax aid to parochial schools.

1. The law requires that every child be educated.

2. Not every parent can educate his own child, so the state, acting for the parent, establishes public schools. The "right" by which the child attends, however, is the parent's, not the state's.

3. The state collects taxes to pay for the education of children, thus creating a common fund for all.

4. Some parents send their children to church schools operated by ecclesiastical personnel.

5. Roman Catholic parents are within their rights in preferring such schools since they meet the state's demand for an educated citizenry.

6. Since Roman Catholics pay taxes into the general fund for public education, Roman Catholic parents are entitled to a fair share of that fund for the maintenance of the schools where they send their children.

7. The religious viewpoint of the educators to whom parents entrust their children is immaterial to the issue of distributive justice. "The doctrine that public aid should be denied by law to certain schools simply on the grounds that they teach a particular religion was never in conformity with the moral canon of distributive justice," states Father John C. Murray.

Distributive justice, then, is the proposition that Roman Catholic parents (or Lutheran, Quaker, or any other preferring religious schools) are entitled to a just distribution of school tax funds for the support of schools of their own choice.

The great importance of natural law to this argument is obvious. First is the primary right of parents over the education of their children. This is a natural law. It might be contended that the education of a child is an affair of both parents and government and that these have equal rights and responsibilities. Roman Catholic theory denies this and affirms that the education of children belongs within the parental sphere.

A second natural law that operates in the Roman Catholic argument is that of fair distribution: government is morally obligated to distribute tax funds to schools of parents' choice in some equitable manner.

There are numerous instances of indirect subsidy to the churches of America in present laws. Clergymen are not required to pay income taxes on the rental value of manses that they occupy free of charge; congregations thus pay less for pastoral services. Church properties are not subject to real estate taxes; churches thus spend money for religious purposes that would otherwise be paid as taxes. With the advantage of such precedents in tax law, Roman Catholics still prefer to argue the school-aid question on the basis of natural law theory. Precedents have only limited force, laws change, but natural law, they hold, is truth and righteousness.

THE ROMAN CATHOLIC VIEW OF CHURCH-STATE RELATIONS

Before attempting a summary of the Roman Catholic viewpoint on the issue of church-state relationships, it is important to recognize certain historical circumstances that have deeply affected the relations of the American Roman Catholic community to the national life.

Roman Catholics entered American life as a minority; many still live in urban concentrations. Roman Catholics are still joined by ethnic ties, principally Irish, German, and Italian. To a "minority mentality" was added the prolonged trial of bitter anti-Roman Catholic prejudice. All this has created a kind of Roman Catholic society in America that has been and remains different from the life of the Protestant majority, although the differences are becoming less marked. The venerable conception of a

"Christian society"—that is, Roman Catholic—has given theological support to the historical reality of a Roman Catholic subcommunity living apart from the generality of American life.

These circumstances have created special problems as the Roman Catholic Church has sought to relate itself to American civil authority. Roman Catholic–Democratic party solidarity in cities like Boston and New York has tended to make Roman Catholic loyalty to church a political loyalty as well. Roman Catholic concentrations of population often induce local public officials to respond to the teachings of the Roman Catholic Church as interpreted by the local clergy. There have been times when anti-Catholicism has been so virulent as to require Roman Catholics to close ranks politically for their own liberty and safety.

Roman Catholic moral theology aside, these circumstances might well have been enough to persuade Roman Catholics to build their own school system. If Protestants regret that they did so, Protestants are partly responsible. While Roman Catholics have shared the cost of educating public-school pupils through taxation, they have borne the cost of their own schools unaided. For several generations, Roman Catholic citizens in effect have been subsidizing the education of non-Catholic children. So long as Protestants ignore such facts as these, there is little likelihood that the present differences on the school-aid question can be reconciled.

Let us now summarize the Roman Catholic viewpoint on church-state relationships.

1. While Roman Catholic theology and social history have produced no political doctrine of religious liberty, American Roman Catholics are in fact committed to the wording of the First Amendment to the United States Constitution.

2. Substantial numbers of American Roman Catholics

agree that the separation of church and state, when construed moderately, is a sound extension of the First Amendment, beneficial to the church as well as to religious liberty.

3. Roman Catholics consider, however, that to construe parochial schools which teach science, civics, language, literature, and history as "church" alone is to distort separation of church and state to the point of social injustice, notwithstanding the fact that such schools are church owned, staffed, and administered.

4. The Roman Catholic view that the spiritual is superior to the temporal implies the superiority of the church to the state. This historic Roman Catholic commitment remains unchanged. In practice, however, American Roman Catholics do not argue that ecclesiastical law should supersede civil law in case of conflict. Roman Catholic doctors, teachers, and administrators in public service as individuals are forbidden to disobey the moral law as the Roman Catholic Church teaches it. Yet they are not taught to impose their religious viewpoint in the performance of public duties. When they do, as occasionally happens, they nevertheless act in conformity with an ancient Roman Catholic teaching based on a union of church and state that never existed in the United States. The Roman Catholic Church has not yet faced this problem theologically.

5. The Roman Catholic Church believes that all societies are grounded in natural law, and to this extent, it seeks a relation of church and state in the United States consistent with its view of natural law. A large body of American Roman Catholic opinion holds that religious liberty is a precept of natural law and that the moderate application of the separation of church and state also has the support of natural law. The precept that error has no rights—a proposition that particularly disturbs Protestants —enjoys formal standing in Roman Catholic moral theol-

ogy but is materially offset by the Roman Catholic view that conscience may not be coerced. Nevertheless, this problem has not been fully resolved in Roman Catholic thought.

Chapter VIII

Strong Separation of Church and State

AMERICANS WHO FAVOR THE FULLEST POSSIBLE SEP-aration of church and state oppose Government aid to all church-related enterprises. They would exclude observances even remotely religious in character from public schools and all religious displays from public property, abolish or secularize Sunday closing laws, and in general carry the separation principle rigorously through a wide range of customs accepted by the American public at the present time.

Some Protestants are very uneasy about tax privileges enjoyed by church and clergy; a few would rather see military chaplains paid by the churches than by the Armed Forces. Sunday closing laws embarrass them; they think church-affiliated hospitals, clinics, and old people's homes should abandon their church ties if they wish to accept state aid.

While Protestants include relatively few strong separationists, Jews, by contrast, are almost entirely at one in desiring a more thoroughgoing separation of church and state. Nonreligious Americans feel almost no sympathy for the moderate and partial separation of church and state that prevails today. If it is not unfair to Mrs. Vashti McCollum to classify her among nonreligious Americans, it might be noted that the famous case that she

67

won not only put religious education off public-school premises but expelled it from scheduled school hours. Since that time, weekday religious education has been conducted only after three or three thirty in the afternoon.

Protestants who favor a more complete separation of religious activities from public programs and financial support do not share Mrs. McCollum's reasons. She wanted to free her child from the embarrassment of being isolated in refusing to participate in the religious education program in Urbana, Illinois. Protestants who favor more separation usually feel that in modern America a scrupulous separation of church and state is the only way to do full justice to persons who disagree with local religious majorities and to keep religion vigorous. Like most Protestants, they reason pragmatically.

The Jewish community supports separation not because Jews disapprove religion and morals—there are few American groups so consistent in their loyalty to community standards as the Jews—but simply because they are a minority that is often imposed upon, sometimes unwittingly, by Christian majorities. Jews feel their identity differently. The strongly orthodox cling to older customs and attitudes and are criticized by more liberal Jews. But almost all American Jews are becoming increasingly conscious of the unique value of their heritage. As a result, liberal Jews are as anxious as the orthodox to be free of the pressure of Christian majorities.

The small number of Americans who are avowedly nonreligious want to live entirely apart from the subtle effects of American religiousness in all its forms. They yield nothing to Christians and Jews in earnest concern for orderly society. But the reasons they act as they do differ widely from the teachings of Jews and Christians, and they demand that public education be uncolored by the national heritage of religious and moral thought. A dedicated handful of militants believes that the welfare of the country demands its total secularization.

Let us attempt to identify separationists by their attitudes toward some of the points discussed in the two preceding chapters.

1. Natural law or positive law?

However they may differ on theory of law, strong separationists come to the same conclusions on church-state relations. If they argue from natural law they conclude that it demands separation of church and state as a prerequisite of political and religious freedom. Those who prefer positive law argue that man controls his own destiny and ought to have learned by now to erect an impregnable wall between religious and civil institutions.

2. What significance has Justice Douglas' observation that "Americans are a religious people" for strong separationists?

Most separationists acknowledge that Americans as a whole are at least superficially religious. Some feel that the general religiousness of the country has real value for the national life but that its benefits can be best realized if church and state are kept strictly apart. Others argue that the question of whether the country is religious or not has nothing whatever to do with its welfare; it is political institutions that are crucial. For the sake of the nation's political integrity, they demand total separation of church and state.

3. What do strong separationists make of the problem of community custom vs. the logic of separation?

Separationists are a logical breed and tend to be impatient with local history and custom. While forced to agree that it may not be practicable in a Roman Catholic community, for example, to take the crucifixes off the classroom walls, or in a solidly Protestant community to put a stop to reading the New Testament in assemblies of pupils, they declare that these things are wrong—which is to say, inconsistent with logical separationism. Some moderate separationists feel that if no injustice is done to any child, the weight of community sentiment is entitled to some recognition, it being understood that if even a single child is forced to undergo indoctrination, the case is quite different. Radical separationists are restless with this reasoning.

Strong separationism sometimes fails to distinguish between separation of church and state and separation of religion and public life. While it is essential to maintain separation between organized churches and civil authority and to exclude the rites and teachings of a single religious group from public programs, it is impossible to extinguish from the mind of a public official his religious and moral convictions or to insist that he should reason from neutral moral principles when deciding matters of state. What we might term a *legitimate* radical separationism demands the total dissociation of all forms of civil authority from church institutions and sectarian practices.

4. What about the specific issue of tax aid for parochial schools?

Separationists of all varieties are unable to accept the Roman Catholic argument that the presence in parochial schools of exclusively Roman Catholic religious instruction, plus ecclesiastical ownership and administration, are immaterial to the question of tax aid. The Roman Catholic reason for this view, that parental right is the regulating principle, not church-state separation, is equally unacceptable to most separationists. If parochial schools were not owned, managed, and staffed by church organizations; and if one religion were not exclusively taught in the curriculum, the question of church and state might be excluded, unless it be further insisted— as some separationists do—that all religious instruction must be eliminated from publicly subsidized education.

Chapter IX

A Protestant Viewpoint and a Provocative Proposal

TO THIS POINT IN THIS STUDY WE HAVE KEPT AS closely as possible to the facts and the problems they pose. Here we will present one man's view of church-state relations. He is a Protestant. What else should be said of his viewpoint we leave to you!

Where should Protestant thought on church-state relations begin?

With the gospel. Not with a specific community problem; not with general principles. These must be considered, but they are not the point of beginning. We must begin with the gospel.

What is the gospel?

The gospel is what God has done among men and said to all of us in order to destroy the barriers that make it impossible for us to know the truth and live by it. *What* God did was to send messengers—lawgivers and prophets—and then to make our life intelligible to us by sending his own Son.

We read in the Bible the testimony of those who knew Jesus. They recount his birth, life, death, and resurrection in order that we, like them, may entrust not only ourselves but also the destiny of the whole world to the divine action that faith sees in the deeds of Christ. All witnesses to this faith belong to the church.

71

What is the church?

The church is not just like other social groups, to be explained in much the same way as the Rotary, the Republican Party, or the local building and loan association. It does not, for example, owe its existence to the decisions of its members to join—although such decisions must be made—but to an act of God. When God sent his Son to call out his own people, he commanded them to believe and obey his Word and to devote their energies to showing clearly by word and life the whole meaning of the gospel. The church is the "body of Christ" partly because the church, like Christ, is something God does. The church is a kind of embassy sent into the world in order to convey God's invitation to life and peace and salvation. It has taken many forms in Christian history: state churches, sects, denominations, even movements without much organization at all. It will take still other forms in the future, but always it will be composed of people who declare that Christ is their Lord, trust in him as their only ultimate hope, and perform his command to witness to the power of his gospel for men and societies.

How does the church regard the institutions of society?

The family, the state, education, social services, the arts, business, and all other social institutions hold special meaning for the Christian man. He believes that when Christ stands before them they are called upon to fulfill the will of the Father.

Take the state, for example. Laws against murder punish murderers; they do not remake them into new men. But once law itself is understood as part of God's total design to redeem us—and this we can believe once we begin to see ourselves and our Government in the light of Christ—even the most minor aspect of civil and personal life takes on new meaning. Family life becomes a sphere of redemption and renewal as well as a sexual union designed for procreation and mutual satisfaction.

The possibility that family, education, social service, state, and church may be definitely related to divine redemption can be realized only by faith. Such faith understands that each of these has its own charter and calling from God. Not one of them—certainly not the church—wholly fulfills the purpose for which God established it. All fail measurably to know and perform their true functions. Yet each has its own dignity and calling and therefore the unique rights, purposes, and limits of each enjoy the full respect of Christians. In relating himself to the social structures, the Christian desires that each of them should fulfill the function for which God established it.

None of these basic structures of society is subordinate to another. The state is not subordinate to church or family; it may not be enlisted in the service of the church or the family or forced to pursue their purposes. It has its own purpose.

Here is our viewpoint in diagram.

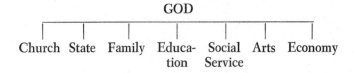

GOD

Church   State   Family   Education   Social Service   Arts   Economy

It is not to the purpose of this brief study to attempt to fix the purposes or number of the basic social institutions. The point is that they differ according to their several purposes; yet since all are united by common service to God, each in a manner peculiar to itself, they exist in *essential* harmony. That they do not always behave harmoniously is not proof that they are fundamentally incompatible but that they are held in balance by continuous mutual criticism and rivalry as well as by mutual service.

Schools in Particular

General education in our kind of society—we must speak specifically to our own situation—we believe is intended by God to convey to new generations a scientific and aesthetic understanding of the whole heritage of human history. Its primary inspiration is the spirit of man.

How schools should be maintained is for circumstance and discretion to decide: by churches or the state, or perhaps by families or voluntary associations or combinations of these. A society's total education system from nursery to graduate school should exclude nothing. However education may be financed, managed, and staffed, it should confer the whole wealth of human experience on the young.

To reduce instruction to indoctrination is to violate the calling of education by bringing it into subjection to a purpose not its own. If, for example, the state uses schools for its peculiar political purpose, it usurps the prerogative of God in education. The tragic quarrels over education in our century reveal a contest between willful men, working through governments and churches, to capture education for their own ends. To do this violates the very character of education.

Separation between the basic institutions is necessary to social and political harmony in the United States. Family, church, state, social service and education, the arts and the economy, are united by God's calling, not by the authority of any comprehensive senior organization, neither the state nor the church. When the state finances schools it ought not purchase control of the curriculum. The same must be said of church sponsorship of education.

The other side of separation is mutual service. Separation between state and school does not mean that the state cannot finance education but that the schools must never be reduced to the service of the state. Separation of state from family does not mean that the state cannot enact marriage, divorce, and adoption laws but that family law must protect the family in the pursuit of its own calling. Separation of state and church does not mean that the state may not make laws that touch the church (for example, law governing property ownership) but that law must guarantee to the churches the fullest possible freedom to pursue their proper calling. Separation of church from state does not mean that the church may not speak and act in civil affairs but that the church never usurps political power but yields the state the full honor due to its calling, encouraging the state to be a true state, not an instrument of the church. A church's reproof is therefore a service to the state, never a usurpation of the state's inalienable right to conduct civil affairs. The state must not and cannot be relieved of responsibility for effective political action. Whether and when, if at all, it will heed the counsels it may hear from church, university, or any other source, only it can say. God alone is the ultimate judge of the state.

Church Action and Cultural Action

Let us now consider the church at closer range. Exactly how does the church relate itself to the other institutions of society?

We discern two basic motives at work within the church: to preach the gospel and to act toward people and institutions as the gospel requires. The first we will term *church action* strictly so-called, since only the church will, can, or ought to preach the gospel. The second we will call the *cultural action of the church,* because concern for the relief of physical suffering, tyranny, family disorder, economic injustice, and other socials ills is shared by persons who acknowledge no specific loyalty to the gospel.

The churches do not always do their jobs well. Whether their failure to clarify the gospel to themselves and others is worse than their failure to act as the gospel requires may be debated. But they have devised different sorts of institutions for these two kinds of action. Preaching the gospel requires worship. A church building is designed for prayer and praise of God and the preaching and teaching of the gospel. A property for these purposes is an adjunct of church action.

Hospitals, schools, or homes for the aged, on the other hand, are institutions designed to enable the church to discharge its responsibilities toward social need in response to its own characteristic motives. They represent the cultural action of the church. Yet institutions of this variety may be as much a concern of the state as of the church.

If church action—worship, preaching, teaching—is forcibly stopped, the gospel is not heard, and this is the church's catastrophe. If the church's cultural action is reduced for lack of funds or taken over by the state, the preaching of the gospel need not suffer, even though a specific kind of action-in-the-gospel may. The church is then sent in quest of new forms of cultural action to meet current needs of society.

Places of worship are principally concerned with *church action* as we have defined it, because they are normally used for activities unique to a church. Among activities unique to the church we must include Christian education: the advocating of specific forms of Christian faith, and the training of teachers and clergymen to advocate Christian faith. Such forms of church education must be distinguished from general education which may also be sponsored by churches.

With church-affiliated cultural services, the situation

is different. Schools for general education have been founded by churches to wipe out ignorance and the evils attendant on it. But the state also has a vital interest in education. General education may be sponsored by any group of people or any social institution. But it remains general education. If sponsored by the state, it does not on that account become subject to the state. When sponsored by the church, it does not become subject to the church. Hospitals, schools, and other cultural services conducted by the churches are not an inherent part of the church in the same way that the gospel is and may not be exclusively regarded as "church" because church sponsored or as "state" because state sponsored. They are unalterably "general education" or "social service."

Worship and theological education, however, is a concern of the church alone. On this reasoning, it is inappropriate for the state to grant tax exemption of property used for these purposes. While the state may assume responsibility for health and education, it ought not assume any financial responsibility for worship.

If, as is happening in the United States, schools, hospitals, and homes for the aged become too expensive for church maintenance and must increasingly depend on tax support, this neither encroaches on the rights of the church nor implicates the state in an improper union with the churches. So long as schools, hospitals, and comparable cultural services remain true to their character, joint support of them by church and state is fully legitimate and entails no breakdown of proper separation of church and state.

The Vexed Question: Roman Catholic Parochial Schools

This line of thought, when applied to the Roman Catholic claim for distributive justice, replaces an old question with a new one. In our view, the charge that separation of church and state is violated when tax aid is given to Roman Catholic and other parochial schools does not meet the real question. If education is a social institution in its own right and not a subordinate department of churches or government, the new question is this: Are church-affiliated schools (all general education) performing their educational task? Are they teaching the whole heritage of human wisdom? Are they opening all the possibilities for understanding, studiously avoiding the limitation of learning, and bringing students into a fully responsible relationship with human history?

Great numbers of private and public schools, particularly Protestant church-related colleges, must take these questions seriously. One contribution to the resolution of the lower school question can come only from Roman Catholics: they must abandon the venerable view that as keeper of the souls of men, the church is superior in authority to all other structures in which men live, including education.

In Roman Catholic theory, not only the state but all social institutions—the family, social service and education, the arts and the economy—are subordinate to the church. With this scheme we contrasted the conception that each human vocation possesses its own mandate from God. The differences between them are not differences of rank or status but of character. Since all callings are of God, they are equal before him.

The proposal here advanced is an invitation to Roman Catholic theologians to undertake a reassessment of their theological understanding of the calling and function of the institutions of society.

Roman Catholic espousal of this view of the relation of the church to other social institutions would not only remove an anachronism of Roman Catholic theory but enable Roman Catholics to set parochial education free from the incubus of indoctrination. When Roman Catholic theologians and their canonical superiors are prepared to grant the equality of the fellowships of men in their several callings under God and apply this principle to the reorganization of parochial education, there will be no theoretical objection to tax aid to church-affiliated schools.

How to Make the Transition

In the United States, education first developed under religious sponsorship. The freedom of education is no better guaranteed by church sponsorship than state support and no better guaranteed by state sponsorship than church affiliation—as professors virulently attacked by sympathizers of the late Senator Joseph McCarthy will testify.

The problem with church-related education has three specific points: (1) It tends toward indoctrination through limitation of curriculum and biased interpretation of general studies. (2) It advocates a single religious viewpoint. (3) It is officially controlled by church bodies.

The state is in position to utilize the power inherent in public assistance in order to free church-related education from these encroachments on educational liberty. This cannot be accomplished in American society by surveillance of teaching personnel. Structural means must be found which will, over a reasonable period of time, produce steady movement toward educational liberty in church-affiliated schools accepting tax aid.

The operative question is: On what terms should the state grant (or continue to grant, as with loans to church-related colleges) tax aid to church-related schools?

We propose the following terms:

1. Church-related schools should dissociate them-

selves from church control so explicitly that they cannot be justly regarded as forms of church action but only as church-sponsored cultural service.

2. The minimal guarantee of educational liberty in schools now church-sponsored should be the transfer of control to a lay board of trustees elected either by the parents of enrolled pupils (in the case of primary and secondary schools) or by a self-perpetuating board (in the case of institutions of higher education), entirely divorced from both official and unofficial ecclesiastical control.

3. Independent boards of trustees should have complete liberty to choose their own managers, adopt curricula, and appoint instructors in counsel with their faculties.

4. No tax-assisted school should be permitted to refuse admission to any applicant on grounds of religious affiliation or require any child to accept religious instruction.

How would this plan actually work?

As regards church-affiliated colleges, the plan would not assure adequate treatment in each college of all religious traditions nor guarantee freedom from bias in every classroom. No plan could accomplish that. But the plan would free boards of trustees to scrutinize their personnel and program from the point of view of education itself rather than their acceptability to church doctrine or authority. Since substantial numbers of colleges are actually sponsored by the major religious groups in America, the total national system of state assisted higher education would be characterized by wide diversity and increasing liberty.

As regards Roman Catholic parochial schools (and all church-related lower schools), the above plan would probably result in the following measures:

1. Since the school would no longer be church-controlled, however closely bound by tradition to the Roman

Catholic Church, it would be eligible for tax support on the same basis as any other private school.

2. The parents of the children enrolled in Roman Catholic schools at the time of dissociation from church control would be entirely Roman Catholic and could be expected to elect an all Roman Catholic board. Such a board could be expected to select an all Roman Catholic faculty and appoint Roman Catholic personnel as managers of the school. (Simply to return the school to diocesan authority would be inconsistent with the plan here proposed.) The board would presumably authorize instruction in the Roman Catholic religion.

3. Since no child could be refused admission on religious grounds, in residential areas of mixed religious affiliation non-Roman Catholic children would eventually enroll. Their parents would then be entitled to vote in periodic school board elections.

4. With non-Roman Catholics represented, the board would be obligated to authorize instruction in other religions, children (i.e., parents on their behalf) being granted liberty to elect their religious instruction.

As with church-affiliated colleges, this plan could not ensure immediate freedom from indoctrination in the classrooms of church-related schools nor furnish instruction in all religious traditions in all schools. The operative principle of religious liberty, however, is that no child should be forced to accept religious instruction. So long as the community remained exclusively Roman Catholic, no child's religious liberty would be violated by a solidly Roman Catholic curriculum and staff. The entrance of a very limited group of non-Roman Catholic children would require, however, that instruction in other religions, as demanded by the affiliation of those children, should be provided and some children might be excused from religious instruction altogether.

The advantages of this plan are these.

1. It would tend to lead schools away from indoctrination and toward the liberty appropriate to education, yet without creating radical immediate change in most communities or involving any policing of schools by civil authority.

2. The state, however, would have the right and duty to review school practices periodically to determine whether a renewal of aid was justified by fidelity to the requirements of the law.

3. The plan would equalize the cost of lower school education among the entire body of taxpayers, regardless of religious affiliation, thus meeting the Roman Catholic claim for distributive justice.

4. The plan would produce an eventual improvement in the quality of primary and secondary education throughout the nation, a prime necessity in the present crisis and an equal benefit to all Americans in itself.

The plan would certainly not satisfy persons who remain convinced that any religious character whatsoever means that a school, hospital, or other agency of cultural service cannot be regarded otherwise than as part of the "church." However, the plan would enable church bodies to withdraw from present cultural services in order to undertake others better suited to their means and skills. They could do this without jeopardizing the continuity and quality of established programs of service. This would apply to hospitals and social services as well as schools.

The plan here proposed definitely affirms the complete propriety of instruction in religion in tax-supported schools. We do not see how the freedom of education can be vindicated when law denies its right to teach any subject. To construe the separation of church and state to mean that public schools may not teach religion is to convert the principle into an instrument of one American subgroup, the irreligiously oriented. There is a small but zealous group of secularizers in the United States who hope to impose their own nontheistic moral values on American children by dominating public education. To many Americans, the separation of church and state is becoming a symbol of a growing intrusion of these particular ideologists on tax-supported education. The fact is that this secularistic philosophy of man is a kind of fourth American religion and its proponents are as bitterly partisan as the most radical Roman Catholic or Protestant religionaires. A truly secular school system must resist this new semireligious encroachment just as sternly as it resists impositions by church organizations or established religious dogmas. If public administrators and judges fail to act in the light of this fact, they will permit public facilities to fall into the hands of a religion of irreligiousness, a matter little different from intrusion by Roman Catholics, Protestants, or Jews. Even to set limits on instruction in religion by law (for example, by authorizing only the cultural and literary study of religion) is to infringe the liberty of education and to allege that it cannot be truly free unless religion and religious interpretations are scrupulously excluded. At the expense of some abuse, it is essential to maintain that whenever education is subjected to artificial restraint of any kind, it is denied its true character.

A QUESTION FOR THE CHURCH

How much justice would a completely free system of public education do religion? Could Protestants expect the school to teach the gospel in its classrooms? Could the Roman Catholic Church look to tax-supported schools, formerly church-controlled, to indoctrinate in Roman Catholic faith?

A competent educational system will do precisely that justice to religion which the purpose of education demands: to lead the student to a scientific understanding of the religious element in the heritage of man. Religion is a different thing to the church than to the school. Churches advocate faith because they believe that without religious commitment men's lives are destroyed. Religion is a part of history but reaches beyond it. Education deals with religion as a historical reality; churches demand that all men face the total question of their destiny.

This is why the Supreme Court's decision prohibiting the New York State public schools from using the Regents' prayer was right *from the church's own point of view*. No civil body has the right to decide what religion shall be taught in tax-supported facilities. Was that prayer a Christian prayer? It scrupulously excluded mention of Jesus Christ, the object of Christian faith and our Intercessor with God the Father. In order to please Jews, it had to. Then what was the religion that underlay that prayer? Not a trinitarian religion but a unitarian religion. It was a prayer of a religion called *deism,* not Christianity. Those who deny God altogether were opposed to it; those who believe that God has made himself known through Jesus Christ ought to oppose it. In attempting to reduce the prayers of three major faiths to a single utterance, that prayer actually defined still another religion—and a very old one—which Christians have resisted from antiquity. Establishing religion is no business of the state. There should be no Constitutional amendment putting the state in the business of religion.

Neither public nor private education ought attempt to duplicate the church's relationship to religion. The church has its own duty to religion as faith and commitment. This it cannot expect the school to fulfill. The church's concern with faith can never fully correspond with the responsibility of education toward religion.

The separation of church and education is a safeguard for both faith and the school, for both the scientific study of the religious heritage of man and the vigorous advocacy of faith. Neither churches nor governments have a right to deny schools the right to teach the religious heritage; nor may churches rely on school or government to advocate faith. Religion belongs to more than churches, but churches are uniquely related to faith.

If religion belongs to history, its place in education cannot be denied by those who fear that the study of religion will give the church an improper foothold in public education. Abuses there will always be, but churches that refuse to grant education its freedom suffer damage to faith as catastrophic as the fate of societies that are afraid to teach their whole heritage.

Questions for Study and Discussion

Chapter I

1. What are the similarities (and differences) between your community and Hightown, U.S.A.? What are the relative sizes of the religious groups in your town? What is the policy of your school board concerning religious observances in the public schools? Does that policy reflect present religious opinion in your community?

2. Do you believe that there is a possibility of conflict in your community? What might Hightown have done to head off its troubles?

3. Who are the opinion makers in your community? Do they work effectively together? Are there differences of outlook between them that would make for factionalism?

4. Where do the Protestant churches of your community stand on (*a*) religion in public education; (*b*) the use of public property for religious displays; and (c) tax exemption for church property?

Chapter II

1. Can you list church-state issues in your community that are potential sources of conflict?

2. What does the word "church" mean to you? What is meant by "sectarian"?

3. What does "state" mean in the United States? Name some "state" powers that touch you through the school dis-

trict (ever had a visit from the truant officer?); the county; the state (what *is* that gas tax spent for?); the Federal Government (now you've had it!).

4. How would you describe your "community tradition" of church-state relations?

Chapter III

1. How do you react to the Hightown settlement? Did it meet Federal Constitutional standards?

2. Is politics a science that can be practiced technically?

3. Can a nation maintain itself without some sort of non-sectarian national religion? What is the difference between a "moral consensus" as a basis for political life and a national religion? Can they exist separately?

Chapter IV

1. From the point of view of the Middle Ages, the separation of church and state was wrong. Why? On what grounds can it be defended as "right"?

2. If it is accepted that neither the unity of church and state nor their extreme separation is good, what are the principles that help the public recognize the right balance between them?

3. Some Christians argue that the church ought to stick to the gospel and let the government take care of politics. What does that mean to you? Complete separation of church and state? Does radical separation mean that churches should pay or not pay property taxes? Does it mean that the church may discuss individual moral questions but not moral issues that touch public affairs? Just what is the dividing line between religion and politics?

Chapter V

1. What is a "Protestant"? Is "Protestantism" a religion? a moral climate? a principle of social grouping? When you

describe yourself as a "Protestant," what do you mean to say? If you say, "I am Catholic" (both Protestants and Roman Catholics may say this), what do you mean by it?

2. This chapter mentions the lunatic fringe. How can the Protestant or Roman Catholic know when some member of his church is going too far? How can churches deal with their own lunatic fringe?

Chapter VI

1. Do you agree with the following points in this chapter? (a) "Almost all Protestants agree . . . that 'we are a religious people.' " (b) "Protestants are pragmatic rather than doctrinaire in their understanding of church-state relations." (c) "Protestants are usually friendly to existing customs."

2. Is birth control moral? Is it intelligent? Should the churches engage in birth control education?

3. What are the policies of your local state or county welfare offices on birth control education?

4. Refer to the chapter summary: Is the state "inevitably involved with moral issues"? Ought morals always "be intimately conjoined with religion"? Are "churches within their rights in discussing moral issues," even in the public realm?

Chapter VII

1. Does the statement of what Roman Catholics believe check out with what you have learned from discussion with Roman Catholic friends?

2. Everybody "feels" things, sometimes quite strongly. How do you rate your moral feelings? Do they reflect the influence of your mother, your digestion, your Scoutmaster, or God? What is conscience?

3. Is there any substance in the Roman Catholic claim for distributive justice? How can distributive justice be reconciled with the separation of church and state?

Chapter VIII

1. Designate someone in your group to advocate radical separation of church and state, another to advocate moderate separationism. For example: Resolved, that our church should pay taxes on all its real property. Or choose another issue from pages 67 to 70.

2. It is common in some parts of the United States to segregate the races. The Supreme Court has ruled against this established custom in public schools. Does community custom have any "rights" or is it simply an obstacle? Granted that custom is a fact, how do you evaluate it, especially when a substantial number of people feel aggrieved or oppressed by it?

Chapter IX

1. "A church's reproof is a service to the state, never a usurpation of the state's inalienable right to conduct civil affairs. . . . Whether and when, if at all, the state will heed the counsels it may hear from church, university, or any other source, only it can say. God alone is ultimate judge of the state." Does this statement define the separateness and the common life of church and state accurately?

2. The Oxford English Dictionary gives the following definition of the word "secular": "of or belonging to the present or visible world; temporal, worldly." On this definition, is the church "secular"? If not, what is a better description?

3. This chapter argues that education is not merely a function of family, state, and/or church but is a distinct institution with its own character, purpose, and right. Can it be argued that education is a *joint function* of family, state, and church rather than an independent "mandate" of God? Is there another theologically adequate and practicable viewpoint?